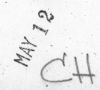

TAPPING
THE
SOURCE

TAPPING

THE

SOURCE

USING THE MASTER KEY SYSTEM
FOR ABUNDANCE AND HAPPINESS

By William Gladstone, Richard Greninger, and John Selby

Foreword by Mark Victor Hansen
Afterword by Jack Canfield
Inspired by the Master Key System of Charles Haanel

STERLING ETHOS
An imprint of Sterling Publishing Co., Inc.

New York / London
www.sterlingpublishing.com

STERLING and the distinctive Sterling logo are registered trademarks of Sterling Publishing Co., Inc.

Library of Congress Cataloging-in-Publication Data Available

10 9 8 7 6 5 4 3 2 1

Published by Sterling Publishing Co., Inc.
387 Park Avenue South, New York, NY 10016
© 2010 by Waterside Productions, Inc.
Distributed in Canada by Sterling Publishing
c/o Canadian Manda Group, 165 Dufferin Street
Toronto, Ontario, Canada M6K 3H6
Distributed in the United Kingdom by GMC Distribution Services
Castle Place, 166 High Street, Lewes, East Sussex, England BN7 1XU
Distributed in Australia by Capricorn Link (Australia) Pty. Ltd.
P.O. Box 704, Windsor, NSW 2756, Australia

Sterling ISBN 978-1-4027-7883-4

For information about custom editions, special sales, premium and corporate purchases, please contact Sterling Special Sales Department at 800-805-5489 or specialsales@sterlingpublishing.com.

CONTENTS

DAILY MANIFESTATION PROCESS

Step 1: Remember to Remember

> *"I choose to focus enjoyably inward."*

Step 2: Quiet Your Mind

> *"My mind is quiet . . . I am now in the Silence."*

Step 3: Enter into Receive Mode

> *"I am open to receive guidance from my Source."*

Step 4: Feel Your Core Passion

> *"I know what I want."*

Step 5: Tap into Manifestation Power

> *"I feel connected with creative power."*

Step 6: Focus upon Your Higher Intent

> *"My vision is right now perfect and complete."*

Step 7: Manifest Your Goal

> *"Each new moment is manifesting my dream."*

*We are always in the presence
of an Infinite and Eternal Energy
from which all things proceed.*

❖

*A single idea may be worth millions of dollars,
and these ideas can only come to those who are
receptive, who are prepared to receive them,
who are in a successful frame of mind. Is it
not worthwhile to make the effort?*

—CHARLES HAANEL,
The Master Key System

FOREWORD

What a treasure you have in front of you in *Tapping the Source*. I know something about manifesting and thinking on a large scale. My Chicken Soup book series has sold more than one hundred and fifty million copies, and I have encouraged and taught tens of thousands of ordinary people just like you to live their dreams and become successful authors and speakers. In *Tapping the Source*, you now have the formula for manifesting your own dreams, whatever they may be. You may be working in the real estate industry, or working as an automobile mechanic, or taking care of your children as a stay-at-home parent. It really does not matter what or if you have a profession because *Tapping the Source* is the key to your true fulfillment and happiness in life. That's right. This book you hold in your hands is all you need to start living the life of your dreams.

Richard Greninger, whom I have worked with as a friend and colleague for more than twenty years, has done us all an enormous service in rediscovering the Master Keys of Charles Haanel and teaming up with William Gladstone and John Selby to create an immediate action plan for twenty-first-century readers not just to read the original keys, but also to implement them. The Focus Phrases and exercises in *Tapping the Source* are unique. No other self-help book gives you these simple exercises that capture the wisdom of the ages and allow you to not just understand how to manifest but also *feel* the energy of manifestation in your very own body.

In studying with my mentor Buckminster Fuller, I was exposed to cutting-edge thought and a mind that was capable of dreaming big dreams. From Bucky I learned to dream big, to dream differently, and to overcome obstacles. With the tools you now have in *Tapping the Source*, I encourage you to dream big, to dream differently, and to overcome the obstacles in your own life. I know you can, and I know that the process of doing so will bring you great joy.

We are living at a unique time in human history. All the technology and building blocks necessary for creating a world that works for everyone already exist. The missing ingredient has been human will and dedication to a larger vision. That larger vision has actually been with us for hundreds of years. Charles Haanel was the first modern thinker to see how to use this ancient wisdom to manifest abundance and happiness. One of my favorite quotes from the Master Key System of Charles Haanel is: "Large ideas have a tendency to eliminate all smaller ideas so that it is well to hold ideas large enough to counteract and destroy all small or undesirable tendencies. This is one of the secrets of success: Think big thoughts. The creative energies of mind find no more difficulty in handling large situations than small ones."

My advice to you is that you use the tools you now have before you in *Tapping the Source* to "think big thoughts." Start with big thoughts and build big dreams. Make them real and share them with humanity. You are here to make a difference.

With my sincere wishes for your highest success,
Mark Victor Hansen

INTRODUCTION

Everything you ever wanted can be yours. Everything. Not just wealth, health, and material abundance but also true eternal happiness.

How can we know this? How can we offer such assurance? What is the source of our knowledge and confidence that this is true?

This book will reveal these secrets in accessible language with easy-to-follow exercises that have proven to be effective. But where did this information come from? Why should you trust that this book is the true guide to all you have been seeking?

In all areas of your life you must always examine the source. This book is not just the creative output of three successful and widely divergent intellects. *Tapping the Source* is first and foremost a modern-day presentation of the ideas provided to the world by an extraordinary individual named Charles Haanel.

Charles Haanel lived from 1866 to 1949. During his lifetime, Haanel created a great fortune and dedicated himself to teaching others his secrets of manifestation. Haanel combined the unique skills of being both a practical businessman and a metaphysician interested in esoteric beliefs and esoteric practices. He was one of the first individuals in America to believe in meditation and manifestation through concentrated focus and discipline. Haanel believed in hard work, but he also believed in something more: the ability of each individual to tap into the Divine Source of knowledge and wisdom that permeates the universe. Of the many books Haanel wrote, his most famous and useful, *The Master Key System*, was published in 1912, almost one hundred years ago. This book went on to influence Ernest Holmes, Napoleon Hill, and many other authors and individuals through to the present day, including the creators of *The Secret*. Anywhere you go on the Internet, you will see the links between Charles Haanel and *The Secret*.

The Master Key System, as a book and correspondence course, sold in excess of two hundred thousand copies at a time when America had perhaps only one-tenth the reading population it has today. One of those readers was a gentleman named Napoleon Hill. Hill is famous for his classic work *Think and Grow Rich*, which has sold tens of millions of copies and is widely regarded as the first and most useful self-help book ever published. He went on to create the Napoleon Hill Institute, which remains robust and active today, still touching the lives of millions of individuals focused on creating material wealth.

Hill wrote a letter in April 1919 in which he gave full credit to Charles Haanel and his Master Key System as the source for his own books and teachings. At this time, Hill had already published the first edition of his book *The Law of Success* and was also publishing his *Golden Rule* magazine, both precursors to *Think and Grow Rich*. In today's world of self-aggrandizing self-help teachers and gurus, this is a truly gracious letter of recognition:

My dear Mr. Haanel:

I believe in giving credit where it is due; therefore, I believe I ought to inform you that my present success and the success which has followed my work as President of the Napoleon Hill Institute is due largely to the principles laid down in *The Master Key System*. I shall cooperate with you in getting your course into the hands of the many who so greatly need your message.

Cordially and sincerely,
Napoleon Hill

Hill was not just a powerful self-help author. He practiced the principles he learned from Haanel and amassed one of the largest fortunes in America through *Golden Rule*, consulting agreements with business titan Andrew Carnegie, and the creation of his own publishing empire. Perhaps even more importantly, he focused on philanthropic activities and sharing his knowledge with others. Indeed even his act of acknowledging Haanel can be interpreted as part of the wisdom imparted in the Master Key System itself. The true power of the Law of Attraction and other laws of abundance that are at the center of the Master Key System is about constantly giving to others and acknowledging the role of others in everyday success on every level of our lives.

Many books, such as *The Law of Attraction* by Jerry and Esther Hicks and *The Secret* by Rhonda Byrne, have taken an idea here and there from the writings of Napoleon Hill and Charles Haanel, but there has never been a book that goes back to Haanel's original words and provides the full context of what his principles and laws really are and how to implement them. Part of the reason for this may be that times have changed since his work was first published, and some of the insights provided are no longer as timely. This in fact is not the case.

Though his writing may seem dated, his ideas are timeless. There is not a single principle or law in the original Master Key System that is less relevant today than when originally published. *The Master Key System* is truly a book of timeless wisdom and insight. The modern world has progressed in many areas in one hundred years, however, and one of the areas of such progress has been specifically in how to use meditation and focused concentration to reach alpha states for peak performance. Books have been written, such as *Flow: The Psychology of Optimal Experience* by Mihaly Csikszentmihalyi and *Zone Tennis* by Jay P. Granat, about how to be "in the flow" or "in the zone" and reach maximum physical and mental potential at all times. *The Secret* hinged on just one of Haanel's principles, but in fact *The Master Key System* illustrates that a single principle from the full twenty-four presented is not sufficient for success.

In *Tapping the Source*, we have gone back to Haanel's original words and principles and have added specific easy-to-follow exercises that enhance your ability to implement Haanel's recommendations. In the original Master Key System, Haanel provided a powerful principle, such as focusing on your connection to the source of abundance in the universe, and then told his readers to sit quietly and meditate on that idea. In *Tapping the Source*, John Selby has developed specific Focus Phrases that mirror Haanel's instructions so that you have a practical guide that will enable you to more thoroughly and more quickly capture the experience of not just understanding but *feeling* what it means to be centered and connected to your ultimate and unlimited potential.

We are humbled to serve as your guides to the wonderful wisdom of Charles Haanel. This is a magical book that will change your life—not just in helping you achieve your own material and emotional desires, but also in helping you help others achieve their goals as well. At the heart of *Tapping the Source* is the awareness that all life is interconnected and that the true secret of happiness is connecting to others and helping them connect to the same Source from which all is manifested. In so doing we all have the potential to live our lives to our fullest potential and to create the conditions for humanity as a collective whole to also reach its highest potential.

As you read *Tapping the Source*, remember to breathe and enjoy.

PART ONE

GETTING STARTED

WHO WAS CHARLES HAANEL?

It is hard to overstate the magic and wisdom of Charles Haanel's life-work. He was a living example of the synthesis of both Western and Eastern philosophies, a man who appreciated material abundance but who never lost sight of the importance of inner calm and inner peace. Haanel was a man with a healthy ego and concern for his own well-being but also a man with tremendous compassion and interest in helping others. He had an innate ability to penetrate the true meaning of world religions and an awareness of the ability of each and every human being to have a direct relationship with the Divine Source of intelligence and abundance that created the universe.

A young Charles Haanel.

Charles Haanel (pronounced *HAH-nell*) was born in Ann Arbor, Michigan, on May 22, 1866, to Hugo and Emeline Haanel. Hugo, like many Americans of his generation, was born in Europe and arrived first in New York City. He relocated to Maryland before moving to Michigan shortly after his discharge from military service in 1862. Hugo married Emeline Fox in 1865, and Charles was born a year later. The family moved to St. Louis, Missouri, when Charles was four years old. Hugo's family was not wealthy and neither was he, but he attended college in Michigan and became the principal first of the Picker School and then of the North School of the Church of the Holy Ghost, both in St. Louis. Hugo and Emeline had four other children, all of whom were brought up in St. Louis. We can deduce from Hugo also having served as a minister that Charles was raised with religious training in the independent Evangelical Protestant traditions of these schools.

Charles was educated in St. Louis, and it was there that he started his business career, quite modestly, as an office boy and then as a clerk for the St. Louis Stamping Company, a Company that perfected the manufacturing of cooking pans. Although records are not definitive, it seems Charles started his work life before the age of fourteen. It is believed he worked for the St. Louis Stamping Company for fifteen years, and by the time he was twenty-nine, he was also president of his own publishing company. At thirty-five, he became the secretary of the Oaxaca Coffee Culture Co., and just four years later—at not yet forty years of age—he was appointed president of the Continental Commercial Company. Continental was a good-sized company with ownership of many sugar, coffee, grape, and cattle plantations spread throughout California and Mexico. At the same time, he was also secretary of the Mexico Gold and Silver Mining Company.

Charles married, at the age of twenty-two, Esther Smith, who bore four children before her untimely death in 1904 at the height of Charles's business success. Charles married Margaret Nicholson of St. Louis in

1908, and Margaret bore him two additional children. Charles died in 1949 at the age of 83, Margaret in 1951. Throughout his business career, Charles maintained an interest in esoteric subjects and was a member of the Keystone Lodge, the Shriners, the Masons, and the Missouri Athletic Club. He was a Republican and a firm believer in the basic family values that he and his family supported throughout their lives.

This seemingly prosaic biography is important for what it doesn't recount: Charles Haanel was a true American. He was not someone who took advantage of others. He was not someone motivated by amassing wealth alone. He understood the common man and woman. He was an entirely self-made business success and rose through the ranks after many years of hard work. He did not just write down his goals and expect them to magically come to fruition. He focused and was disciplined in seeking knowledge and working one day at a time toward success. Nor was he immune to tragedy—not only did his first wife die prematurely, but one of his daughters also died while still a child.

Throughout his life, however, Haanel was obsessed with learning and sharing information with others. He started his first publishing venture while still in his twenties and perhaps while still working as a clerk for the St. Louis Stamping Company. It was during this time that Haanel developed, first as a correspondence course, the Master Key System that is the inspiration for *Tapping the Source*. Haanel went on to write many other books, some of them related to his interest in meditation and Eastern religions. However, none of the books written after *The Master Key System* come close to the power contained in those courses and the eventual book first published in 1917.

Some have speculated that the Master Key System was first created to be shared only with elite business leaders and those with the sophisticated educational background that Haanel himself did not have. We do not believe that was the case, though clearly it was not until Napoleon Hill and others started to publicly acknowledge their debt to the Master Key System that Haanel became a popular public figure. However, even before the Master Key System was published as a book accessible to all, Haanel had already achieved a position of prominence and esteem in St. Louis society. Writing in *St. Louis: The Fourth City* (St. Louis: S. J. Clarke Publishing Company, 1909), author Walter B. Stevens introduces us to Haanel, stating:

> Charles Haanel is largely associated with the business interests of the city, being affiliated with a number of enterprises of acknowledged financial worth. . . . Mr. Haanel is in every sense of the word a self-made man, having risen in the commercial world to his present situation of worth and prominence by the utilization of his own natural resources.

This is not from an obituary, but from a book about the history of St. Louis at a time when Haanel was not yet forty-five years old. This was also written at a time when very few, if any, people knew of the Master Key System. This is important, since so many of today's self-development and get-rich-quick gurus are getting rich only on the advice they are providing and not on the actual experience of creating real value in agriculture, manufacturing, mining, and industry as Haanel had prior to ever writing about or sharing his secrets to wealth creation.

Stevens concludes his entry on Haanel for the 1909 publication with perhaps the most succinct and complete overview of Haanel ever written:

> He is a man of mature judgment, capable of taking a calm survey of life and correctly valuing its opportunities, its possibilities, its demands, and obligations. He has wisely sought success along the lines of least resistance, and yet, when difficulties and obstacles have confronted him, he has displayed a force of character that has enabled him to overcome them and continue on the pathway to prosperity.

Many a man whose life is one of untiring industry does not win success for he lacks the complement to industry a laudable ambition which prompts the individual to reach out into other fields and eagerly grasp the opportunities that are presented. In these qualities Mr. Haanel is richly endowed and has thus attained his present enviable position in financial circles.

The key points for us, as advocates of Haanel, is to recognize that he was a truly self-made man and one whose "laudable ambition" prompted him to "reach out into other fields and eagerly grasp the opportunities." We do not believe from examining Haanel's life and work that these ambitions were limited to financial interests only. Why would a man who, at the age of forty-four, had already achieved such remarkable financial success and recognition dedicate so much of his time and energy to creating the Master Key System and sharing his success secrets with others? In part it could be just good business practice, for, as Haanel has written in the first explanation ever formulated of the Law of Attraction, giving to others is the key to attracting, but it seems more likely that Haanel's having achieved a high level of material and emotional happiness in his own life was sincerely motivated by an altruistic impulse to help others.

Because this book is called *Tapping the Source*, it is essential that you know the source of the information you are reading. Haanel, in our opinion, is an impeccable source. And, just as you have read, it is not just our opinion, but also the opinion of Napoleon Hill and many other self-made millionaires and self-development teachers. For many, Haanel is considered to be "the Father of Personal Development," and we as authors of *Tapping the Source* fully agree. But before you go forward in your reading of our presentation of the modern, up-to-date, enhanced-power version of the Master Key System that *Tapping the Source* is meant to be, you should also know something about Richard, William, and John, your guides to the brilliant teachings and techniques of Charles Haanel.

❖ 2 ❖

WHO ARE RICHARD,
WILLIAM, AND JOHN?

❧❧❧

O kay, so Charles Haanel was an extraordinary and extraordinarily accomplished human being. But what does that matter to you? Well, it so happens that the techniques that Haanel developed actually work and have worked for millions of people over the last one hundred years. Even more important, there are profound and practical insights Haanel shares that will help you no matter what your position in your life, your educational background, or your personality type. This is what is truly extraordinary. Most self-help authors and teachers provide information and techniques that are useful for certain types of individuals and certain types of thinking. Haanel's Master Key System, unlike any of the other dozens of systems we three authors have ever studied or used, is truly universal.

You could not find three more divergent personalities than your author team of Richard Greninger, William Gladstone, and John Selby. Each of us has been extremely successful in aspects of our lives. Each of us, upon studying Haanel's Master Keys, achieved personal mastery in our own lives when we followed the guidance provided in his book. And based on what we know now, we have come together to share what we each believe is the simplest and most powerful guidance any human being can have toward living a happy and successful life.

RICHARD GRENINGER

Richard Greninger never thought that he would be an author or teacher. Richard attended the prestigious Art Center College of Design in Pasadena, California, which is known the world over for developing famous world-class photographers, filmmakers, and automobile designers. Richard's commercial career began in 1970, and he was a commercial producer in Hollywood for some fifteen years. As his career progressed, he became familiar with the personal development field of production. He was introduced to Berny Dohrmann, founder of CEO Space and a visionary in transforming people's way of thinking, and was asked to create live videos for a self-help seminar called IBI. IBI was about teaching people how to create multiple streams of income. Among the speakers who spoke at these seminars were the creators of the Chicken Soup for the Soul book series, Mark Victor Hansen and Jack Canfield, and many other self-help gurus and inspirational speakers. As it turned out, Richard had a wonderful ability to capture Mark and Jack's presentations and their audiences in a way that grabbed people's attention. Word spread, and soon Richard was the go-to videographer for Tony Robbins, T. Harv Eker, and many other motivational speakers.

Richard's videography business thrived, and along the way Richard could not help but notice that the basic messages of many of these speakers were similar and that the people attending were not coming just to increase their incomes, but also to be inspired and motivated to live happy and fulfilling lives. The energy at many of these events was extraordinary, and Richard was able to observe firsthand the near-miraculous transformations and successes of many who had attended. But Richard also observed that in many cases the same people would return again and again, even after achieving success, still seeking more profound results or simply because they enjoyed being in the energy created at these events. Why was that so?

Richard, being someone who wants to know why things work, started to study on his own. In the process, he came upon the work of Haanel and his Master Key System. Haanel was a revelation for Richard. Here, in one small book, were all the keys that all of the other self-help teachers were talking about. Richard became so motivated that he created his own very basic video version of the Master Key System and started living the principles in his daily life. Although the video series did not take off at that time, Richard felt and saw the powerful success these tapes had with those who viewed them. He vowed then that, when the time presented itself, he would find a way to bring the wisdom of the Master Key System to millions of people through a book and a new and better video series. Of course, one of the major problems for Richard was that he was not an experienced writer. And so he waited.

WILLIAM GLADSTONE

As John Lennon wrote, "Life is what happens when we are busy making other plans." One of Richard's other plans was to work on a promotional video for a novel by a friend of Mark Victor Hansen's, William Gladstone. The novel was called *The Twelve*, and part of the assignment included flying to New York City to shoot some subway scenes with William. In the process, Richard and William became good friends. Shortly after the promotional video for *The Twelve* was completed, Richard drove down from his home and studio in Newport Beach, California, to William's home and office in Cardiff by the Sea, California, to go over the final cut and make some tweaks. The meeting turned into lunch, and after lunch Richard mentioned to William that his own dream—much like the writing of *The Twelve* had been William's—was to write and publish a major book acknowledging Charles Haanel and his Master Key System as the most powerful self-help guide ever written.

William was busy with many other projects in addition to promoting his novel. As the founder and active president of Waterside Productions, a major literary agency, he was personally representing best-selling authors such as Eckhart Tolle and Neale Donald Walsch. However, William could not ignore the enthusiasm with which Richard raved about Haanel and his Master Key System. Finally, with some reluctance, William gave in. "Okay, send this Master Key System to me and I will see what I can do. We will need to bring in a writer to update the story for twenty-first-century readers, but if the original is as strong as you say it is, I am sure I will be able to find a writer."

A few days later, the manuscript of the original Master Key System arrived. William was too busy to do more than spend about five minutes with it, but he thought a local writer he was meeting with that very day might be ideal to rewrite the text. So William gave this writer the manuscript with the hope that he would be inspired to become part of the project. The writer took about a week before responding to William, and though he was excited by the material, he had another project that required his immediate attention. It looked unlikely that he would be able to even consider becoming the coauthor of a book about the Master Key System for another five or six months. That was just too long to wait, so William had the writer return the manuscript and decided he would take it with him the following weekend when he went to Kauai, Hawaii, for his annual spring vacation.

William is not your ordinary literary agent. He grew up in a wealthy book publishing family and wanted to be a writer before his father persuaded him that writing was an unlikely profession if he ever expected to support a family or maintain the highly affluent lifestyle he had experienced as a child. William had obtained an advanced degree in cultural anthropology at Harvard University before entering the world of business, and from his first days as a film producer working with Rod Serling and NBC Television, and then as an executive editor for Harcourt Brace Jovanovich Publishing, it was clear William had a unique talent for selecting and managing creative talent. William is always focused, disciplined, and a hard worker. Utilizing these Haanel-like qualities, as well as his natural openness to "synchronicity" and "good fortune," William soon built his own multimillion-dollar literary agency, Waterside Productions, which not only represents book authors but entire companies, including mid-level mergers and acquisitions up to $30 million in individual transactions. William is a busy guy but believes in living a balanced life that includes playing golf and taking frequent visits to his second home in Kauai.

JOHN SELBY

One of the friendships William had developed in Kauai was with an author named John Selby. John is an accomplished writer and has worked with a number of literary agents in order to build his résumé, which includes more than twenty books with more than a million copies sold in total. The relationship between William and John sometimes included some agenting, but William is not John's primary literary agent and their relationship is based more on having children with similar interests and both having received Ivy League educations (William went to Yale as an undergraduate, John to Princeton).

John knew William was coming to Kauai that May and had invited William to dinner soon after he was due to arrive. A funny thing happened to William on the plane ride from San Diego to Kauai. He read Haanel's original *The Master Key System* cover to cover. He couldn't believe the manuscript. He later commented to Richard and John, "I felt that I was reading a manuscript that I could have written myself. I have been living these principles in my work for the last twenty-five years. Haanel's Master Keys are literally the keys to my own career and financial success."

Well, the dinner with John took a very different course than just talk about the kids and John's latest marvelous video products, which were designed to help people sleep better and reduce stress. "John, you have got to read this manuscript. I need a writer to bring this up to the twenty-first century, and in my gut I know you would be great for the task," William suggested, almost before dinner had started.

John replied, cheerfully but firmly, "Well, I'm super busy with my new video production and I have another agent who is offering me a book deal, so I really just don't have the time. I'm sorry, but at this stage of my life I really want to focus exclusively on my own projects."

Never one to give up on creative talent without a second or third attempt, William simply looked at John as he handed him the manuscript. "I understand," William said, "but please at least skim this and let me know if you can think of someone else on the island I might meet with. I know this is powerful and deserves a great writer like you."

"Okay, I can do that at least," John responded as he took the manuscript and noticed that it was the work of Haanel. "Funny you should hand me this. My grandfather was a major cattle rancher and owned the largest ranch in what is today Ojai, California, and he used to rave about Charles Haanel and his Master Key System to me when I was a boy. I never paid much attention at the time, but I did come across his work later when I was doing my studies in cognitive psychology at Princeton. It will be good to spend an hour or two getting reacquainted with Charles and his Master Keys. Must be more than thirty years since I looked at his stuff."

Dinner in John's Kauai "writing shack" was even more pleasant than usual that evening, with great barbequed steak prepared by John and exotic, organic Hawaiian vegetables, grown and prepared by John's wife, Birgitta. When William woke up the next day, he was pleased but not altogether surprised when John called, almost shouting, "This is unbelievable. In the last thirty years, my entire life's work has been on helping people focus and overcome addictions and stress. Now I see that I have been missing one major ingredient in my own teaching, and Charles Haanel has had that secret for me all these years. There is no question. I was meant to write this book. My heart is racing just thinking about what a powerful message we can bring to others and how I can use my expertise in teaching breathing meditation exercises to fully complement what Charles Haanel has been recommending for more than a hundred years. I know I have the missing ingredient that will enable people to immediately use the Master Keys in a way that they never could before. When should we get started?"

And of course John was 100 percent correct. The book you hold in your hands is the result of the unique gifts of three different authors. We are certain that what you will discover is the most inspiring and practical advice you will ever read anywhere: the original and streamlined wisdom of master thinker and manifester Charles Haanel.

❖ 3 ❖

How to Use This Book

~❦~

As three very different authors with different learning styles of our own, we recognize that not all readers should necessarily read books in the same way. For those of you who are able to immediately start working with the core material from Charles Haanel and can jump into the meditation and breathing exercises provided, go directly to part two, "Activate Your Inner Potential." Just read along page by page through to the end, making certain to actually do the exercises in the order they are presented. John Selby has helped tens of thousands of people with exercises similar to those provided, and the unique context of Haanel's Master Keys and insights will ensure success if you follow the program John has created.

For those of you who are hurried for time or just not ready to sit down for a long read that includes doing the exercises, it is fine to start with the insights provided by Richard and William. In fact, for some of you, that may be all you need—just a reminder in simple language of what really matters in life and how to be happy and successful (and rich in financial terms as well, if that is important to you).

Those of you interested in business may just want to start with chapter 5, which has the distilled business principles William first wrote about in his own business autobiography, *Be the Deal*, which he later recognized as resonating so closely with the Master Keys of Haanel.

Other readers—especially those who have been exposed to concepts such as the Law of Attraction, the Law of Abundance, and other principles

Richard writes about based on his own interpretation of Haanel's Master Keys and what he has learned from his decades-long association with Tony Robbins, Mark Victor Hansen, Bob Proctor, and other teachers—may want to start with chapter 4, immediately following this section.

Some of you may want to jump to part four, "Practice Makes Perfect." Although these are in fact the final words, they are also a synthesis of the key phrases and insights from Haanel's Master Key System. John, William, and Richard have found a way to represent these teachings in a way that will be immediately useful to your everyday lives. If you do nothing more than read and reflect upon these final ten pages of *Tapping the Source*, you will have received more than your money's worth from purchasing this book. And if you are able to absorb the incredible wisdom and put into action the insights from these ten pages of "final words" from Haanel, consider yourself ready to become a guide and teacher to others as well.

Of course, most people will benefit greatly from reading and implementing John's Focus Phrases. John's phrases and meditation teachings are the secret missing ingredient. So, if you are like most people, simply read the rest of the book exactly as we have written it. Our authentic desire in writing *Tapping the Source* is to help you and others create a better world. We are living in a time of both individual and collective crises, and *Tapping the Source* is designed to be but one of many resources to help you respond to the challenges that may face you and those you love.

John was the primary writer for parts two and three of *Tapping the Source*. He sometimes writes in the first person, and sometimes not. Conceptually and editorially, *Tapping the Source* is a collaborative effort on every level, and all three authors have incorporated their unique knowledge into the material that awaits you.

❖ 4 ❖

RICHARD'S BACKGROUND AND INSIGHTS

ince 1989, I have been privileged to work with the top masters of the personal development world as a producer of their large seminars and video media: Tony Robbins, Mark Victor Hansen, Jack Canfield, Bob Proctor, and so many other great intellects. One of my jobs was to interview attendees for the all-important "testimonial moment" in each video. It struck me that I kept interviewing the same people over and over again. And so I asked myself, "What did they miss at the last event that they felt they needed to attend the same program again?"

These programs promised participants newfound wealth, fame as an author or speaker, and a great career as an entrepreneur in the world of business. Some promised a new and exciting connection to their primary relationship, and maybe even finding a true soul mate. So what did each of these individuals hope to find? Did they really want to travel the hard road of becoming an author, or risk everything to start a new business, or trade in their current relationship for a new model? Why were these people exploring these workshops for information they could use to change their lives for the better? What were they *really* looking for?

What I discovered is that they all had one thing in common: They wanted to be happy and content. All the aforementioned desires were just a means to that end: to be happy and have time to enjoy their life with some sense of balance. That is why *Tapping the Source* was written: to give you a road map to the destination of personal happiness.

My goal is to bring you and your loved ones a new point of view on how to achieve happiness. When you think that happiness is a state of mind, then why can't we just be happy? If you look at people around the world, they find happiness with or without money, power, and prestige. People are happy most everywhere, and they don't necessarily have a financially free life. They work, eat, and find happiness in their everyday lives. Quite frankly, having millions in the bank is less important to me than living like a millionaire. I would be pleased if this book generates millions of dollars, but trust that I will not allow managing additional wealth to take my time and energy away from the things that have proven to be my true source of happiness. Having time to share with loved ones and do the little things with them can be worth more than a million bucks!

If you follow the path that John, Bill, and I have laid out, while gleaning the amazing wisdom of Haanel as your GPS to destination happiness, I can promise that you will find what you are looking for. I am not guessing. This is an absolute guarantee. You can and will find happiness. All I ask is that you pass this book on or, better yet, buy several and give them to your friends; that way they will be with you when you arrive at destination happiness. Good luck!

USING THE LAW OF ABUNDANCE

Abundance. Well, I have to tell you that I am tired of hearing about all the abundance in life when around me is lots of lack of it, or so it seems. You have to ask yourself, "If there is so much abundance, then where is it? It isn't in my bank account!"

Therein lies the problem: Abundance never shows up in the form of paper. It shows up as satisfaction, smiles, happiness, pride, and prestige. The paper stuff is just a calculator of your abundance, and not necessarily the real thing.

Money fundamentally represents the fruits of your labor, what you actually love to do. Your passion is what drives you and moves you to your finest moments. This personal movement creates success and fame, and the resulting output is wealth in all of its forms. If you chase money for money's sake, the result may be paper money, but that money may not track with true abundance.

The Law of Abundance shows itself at work everywhere. It is wise to stop and take a look at what is really around you. Glance at nature, billions of stars, millions and millions of trees, flowers, plants, animals, fish, and people. There is no shortage here, and even if there were, nature can replenish and reproduce at will.

The shortage we are feeling can be corrected by carefully using the laws of nature to bring to you what you truly desire. Haanel stated it this way: "The law is that THOUGHT is an active and vital form of DYNAMIC ENERGY which has the power to HARMONIZE AND CORRELATE with the mind's vision and creations. Then it brings out from the invisible world; substance from which all things are created and then ultimately delivered into the visible or physical world." It is pretty powerful and exact, not a lot of guessing going on in the universal design.

As you look at the broad landscape of life, you soon will come to the realization that all this came from somewhere, and it wasn't purchased at the local mall. Every material possession you own—your car, your house, your golf clubs—comes from the infinite invisible where everything exists in a form of moving energy. I recently did a Google search for "images of atoms," and there they were, moving atoms under a powerful electron scope. Energy is the substance from which all things are created, and that includes you, your future, and the things that support you. The law operates on vibrations, and that is why you must have the convincing emotion and desire in your body and mind to harmonize with the Law of Vibration, which will bring forth your desires as your vision has created them. Dream on!

USING THE LAW OF VIBRATION IN YOUR DAILY LIFE

The most mysterious and profound event of all time had no apparent cause. Nothing in science or language can adequately describe what occurred in that first hundred-millionth of a second when the majesty of an intelligently designed universe suddenly came into being.

Everything that exists in the universe, even the cold vacuum of empty space, vibrates in a kind of never-ending cosmic dance.

Whether we can see it or not, everything is constantly shimmering, jiggling in its own rhythm. This includes humanity's magnificent ancestral home. The earth and everything on it continuously pulsates to its own unique vibration. Everything that exists vibrates.

Let me see if I can clearly demonstrate to you how all this works in our real world. When you turn on a radio, your antenna attracts the station that you want to listen to. In reality, your antenna transmits the same pulse that the large radio station on the hilltop transmits. These radio pulses harmonize when they bump into each other, just as two instruments vibrate when they are in tune. This signal is called the carrier signal.

Amazingly enough, when the two radios are connected with the carrier signal, you can send messages from one station to the other by pulsing the carrier. It sounds a little complicated, and it is. However, if you step back you can see that your body is like the radio, looking for a connection to the great radio in the sky, your Creator.

Your unique vibratory rate can connect with your Creator, and you download what you need to create your vision. Metaphysics in a nutshell! Does it take a leap to go with it? Sure, just like it does to believe your cell phone is talking to a local cell site 24/7 from your pocket—unbelievable but true. So, may I suggest that it is just a nice way to move through life? You connect and you receive . . . why not?

USING THE LAW OF WEALTH IN YOUR DAILY LIFE

It is essential to understand the nature of wealth, how it is created, and what it depends on. Understand that success is contingent upon a higher ideal than men and women accumulating riches. True wealth depends upon man's creative ability and the application of these abilities in the real world.

It is valuable to understand that premature wealth, the type some-times experienced by a lottery winner, can be the forerunner of personal and financial disaster. This disaster usually happens because the receiver has not understood the Law of Wealth, and the results are obvious.

Wealth is a product of labor. Capital is an effect, not a cause; a ser-vant, not a master; a means, not an end. Money is a result of work, and when there is no work involved, the value of the capital has no reference point, and that is the case with premature wealth.

Hence, wealth should never be desired as an end, but simply as a means of accomplishing an end result. Success is contingent upon a higher ideal than a mere accumulation of riches, and those who aspire to such success must formulate an ideal for which they are willing to strive. Another way to say this is: If you have a big enough "why," then the "how" will be provided naturally.

The power to create depends primarily upon spiritual power. Ideal-ization, visualization, and materialization are three essential steps in this process. Thought always precedes any action, and that action is always a result of thinking. How you act is a result of how you think, and as you think, you become. Therefore, it is critical that your thoughts remain under your control, and these thoughts will guide your actions until you achieve your desired goal.

We can form our own mental images without regard to any limitations of budget, place, circumstances, or the like. These building blocks must be protected from the negative thoughts that surround each of us every day. These negative thoughts always enter our mind through the five senses of the body. Environment, chance, and fear of failure are powerful negative energies that should be contained and kept out of the creative process.

If we can form our own mental images via our process of thought, regardless of what others may think, of exterior conditions, or of environ-ment, then we can control our own destiny, body, mind, and soul—all this by exercising the power of the mind.

Therefore, to control thought is to control circumstance, conditions, environment, and destiny. This is the key to creating wealth. These natural laws work in a perfectly natural and harmonious manner; hence, everything seems to "just happen."

So, if you wish to bring about the realization of a desire, form a mental picture of such by repeatedly visualizing and, most important, feeling your desire. Feel what it is like to be there now, and, like the antenna on a radio, send out to the invisible world a request to provide you with what you need to create that worthwhile desire.

THE POWER OF THINKING—WHAT A THOUGHT!

It is has been said that thinking is what separates you and me from all the other people in the world. Thinking is unique to each of us, somewhat like a fingerprint. Did you know that even identical twins from the same egg have different fingerprints? They say that your fingerprint is the unique spiritual address of your mind—what a thought!

The question is, how do we embrace all the wonderful opportunities that the world has to offer and at the same time be a unique individual? Each of us has many of the same goals as others, so how do we achieve without becoming just another face in the sea of humanity? How do we climb above it all to reach what we see as our destiny? The answer is clear: Use the power of your perfect mind.

Haanel was the personal teacher of Napoleon Hill, who wrote *Think and Grow Rich*. To quote Haanel, "How we think is who we become." Therefore, it is vital to respect our thoughts as a creative force for our future. Everything ever made in the world came from a thought. Thoughts are things and must be treasured as such.

Creating a fulfilling life is much like driving a car. There are rules of the road, and if you obey the rules you will probably have fewer accidents than if you chose to ignore them. Our Creator has seemingly created some very clear rules that drive each of us on a moment-by-moment basis.

There are many laws of nature, including the Law of Attraction, the Law of Wealth, the Law of Health, the Law of Power, the Law of Morality, the Law of Spirit, and the Law of Vibration.

Knowing how these laws operate will affect your personal journey. Achieving a balanced life is a product of using nature's laws to your advantage. Again, these are nature's laws, not some personal or organizational law that will change; these are fixed, permanent laws. Test it out for yourself: Try to change, say, the Law of Gravity. See what I mean?

Each of us has a brain, which is a physical organ of the body. The brain receives signals from your nervous system and gives you messages as to whether you are on the smooth path of life or on a path that leads to anxiety and turmoil. The Law of Morality will be the first red light indicator on the dashboard that will get your attention when you divert from an honest and worthwhile direction.

Tapping into the source of your creation is essential for you to receive the power and insight from your Maker. I would imagine he or she or it is perfect in all ways, so it would seem to me that if that same life force made you and me, then you received everything you need to discern the marvelous possibilities that are all around us. We can take control of our natural gifts and power to make our hopes and dreams come true. Your thinking is what will guide you to your destiny, and *Tapping the Source* is the perfect road map to your great adventure. Let's go!

YOUR SPIRIT: A CHOICE POINT

Throughout history, mankind has been seeking a true purpose for being here on planet Earth. We have been seeking, creating, hoping, praying, kneeling, envisioning, and for that matter dreaming of a place that makes everything worthwhile and fulfilling.

I believe that we as humans have what I call a "choice point." We have an opportunity to play the game, join the crowd, mingle with the believers—or not. The "or not" part is pretty scary, since 90 percent of all humans seek solace in a higher power. You can venture down the path of life with the faithful or choose to make it on your own.

I think I would recommend the choice point of spirit. My father is ninety years old as I write this, and he is a nonbeliever. I say to him, "Dad, if you are right and there is nothing after this, then who cares? If you are wrong and there is a great afterlife when we pass on, then you probably would have wished you had chosen a different path."

The point is, there is no downside to choosing a spiritual path. Beliefs in a spiritual world have been around a very long time, and that alone has to be something to look into. If you feel more comfortable looking toward a third-party entity such as Jesus, God, Buddha, Allah, or any of the hundreds of images we choose to follow, or you are more inclined to a metaphysical belief in which you are part of the Creator, then fine.

Make a choice and enjoy the benefits that come with being part of a group of like-minded people, most with good intentions and a view of a better life ahead. Don't worry about proving to yourself that "this is it"— sometimes looking for proof is a waste of time. Like your radio, you don't need to figure out what makes it work; just turn it on and enjoy it, and you probably won't go wrong.

Having a spiritual connection opens many doors. Haanel said this about spirit:

> Spirit, whatever else it may or may not be, must be considered as the essence of consciousness, the substance of mind, the reality under-lying thought. And as all ideas are phases of the activity of conscious-ness, mind or thought, it follows that in spirit, and in it alone, is to be found the ultimate fact, the real thing, or idea.

Spirit is creative in its purest form, and we humans have the one thing that separates us from all other creatures on the planet: We are creative.

Spirit is the ultimate creative force and exemplified by our existence. So, to bottom line it, I say, "Go with it!"

MANAGE YOUR OWN MEDIA

In the last several decades, new forms of media have invaded our daily lives. First there was television, then two hundred channels of cable, interactive fiber-optic cable, streaming media from computer networks, and now iPods are connected to every ear in America. Blogs, Twitter, MySpace, and Facebook keep us all connected in some form or another. Every moment seems to be documented, talked about, and viewed by strangers for one purpose or another.

Certainly these wonderful technological discoveries are extraordinary and have brought a world of entertainment and information to every facet of society. Celebrities seem to guide our buying habits, our political views, and even our personal dreams and aspirations.

Society seems to live vicariously through *The Oprah Winfrey Show*. We wake up to Regis and Kelly so we can prepare what we will talk about around the water cooler at the office.

We are glued to news of Britney and Jessica, as their lives make radical turns to the altar or the bedroom, and then off to the courtroom.

The nightly news puts us to bed with seemingly unending chaos, human tragedy, and heart-wrenching hopelessness.

The question I ask is, What about you? What about your life? What does this barrage of information and images do to inspire, motivate, and uplift your life in a world that is already difficult to navigate?

How do you become sensual and passionate while body bags are being counted and RPGs are mutilating our eighteen-year-old soldiers on the flat screen above your bed?

How do you feel accomplished when there are images everywhere idealizing the latest hot car, sprawling estate, outrageous destination, or beautiful men and women made even more unattainably so by the magic of Photoshop?

How do you move forward in your personal life when it seems that everyone has already arrived—and become a millionaire?

I think you get the point, and the point is: It is time that you lived for *you*, *your* life, *your* dreams, and *your* rewards.

Often, the source of satisfaction and dissatisfaction is comparison. What we compare ourselves to is critical to our personal happiness meter. If you compare your financial success to that of Bill Gates every morning, I can assure you that you will feel like a pauper even if in reality your financial profile is one to be admired. Again, if you compare yourself to Naomi Campbell or Tom Cruise in the looks category, well, you will have to spend a lot of time at the gym and in front of the mirror with little satisfaction.

Tapping the Source teaches that you can start a process of listening to your inner self, your true partner in life. Begin to use this deliberate form of communication, which is not really new, but an approach you might have put on the shelf a long time ago.

We can begin this journey with the suggestion of shutting off, unplugging, and disconnecting. Go offline. What a thought! It almost sounds like treason these days.

Think of it: simply being with the one you love in a calm and quiet atmosphere. Maybe you have a nice light dinner, with candles burning, and you sit next to each other with absolutely no expectations, just sit with each other, in the silence . . . simply being together. You don't have to be cute or charming or smart or sharp or witty or funny. Just try to be with each other.

You will find that it is an eye-opening and maybe even sensual experience of the highest quality. When you tap your inner source, you will find an extraordinary place to create memorable moments that you can develop and share with your loved one. A new form of communication will appear that will touch each other's hearts—that is, if you don't touch the flat screen remote. Try it. I think that if you manage your media intake, you might just save your life.

Your Source of Your Health Is You

Understanding that your physical body reacts to your mental state helps to develop a lifestyle that is healthy. Thoughts can bring about an emotional vibration that can be helpful or harmful to the physical body's response.

The life force process is carried on by nutrition, secretion, and elimination. This process includes the complexities of the how, why, and what of food and drink. How is the food prepared and emotionally ingested?

How does eating relate to your hunger, fuel, health, and emotional habit? What to eat and drink brings the thought vibration into the body. Creating nurturing feelings, thoughts, and food can bring your senses to a state of well-being and an emotional vibration of wellness.

Every mental action is a vibration. Any given vibration, therefore, immediately modifies every atom in the body affecting every life cell.

The objective mind has certain effects on the body that are readily recognized: laughter, tears, or blood rushing to the face when angry or embarrassed. It is amazing how the mental state affects the body through the emotional vibration of joy, sadness, fear, and elation.

The action of the subconscious mind differs. When wounded, thousands of cells begin the work of healing at once. A surgeon sets a broken bone, but it is the subconscious mind that restores the bone. The subconscious mind will build a wall around an infection to facilitate healing. Using the vibration of perfection and wellness, the subconscious mind is aided by the superconscious mind to restore perfection.

Thoughts make a difference. Each cell in the body carries intelligence. Cells are known to respond to thought, and positive thought can enhance healing. Every element of the human body is the result of the rate of vibration. Mental action is a rate of vibration. A higher rate of mental vibration governs, modifies, controls, changes, as well as destroys a lower rate of vibration. Therefore, understanding the power of the mind can allow us to be harmonious with the always present natural laws. Everything in the universe is what it is by virtue of its rate of vibration. Everything and everyone is using this power to sustain life.

You can enhance becoming your ideal self by connecting with the Originating Mind that forms, upholds, sustains, and creates all there is. This is the essence of *Tapping the Source.*

❖ 5 ❖

WILLIAM'S BACKGROUND AND INSIGHTS

※

I n 1998 I wrote a book titled *Be the Deal*. This book was written in ten days and never edited, but was immediately rushed to print within thirty days of having been written. *Be the Deal* was the first individually authored book ever to be published by ToExcel, the forerunner of iUniverse, which is now part of Author Solutions. We believe that *Be the Deal* may be the first book ever published using print-on-demand technology, and the purpose of the book was actually to prove the concept that print on demand could be used effectively to create commercially viable books cost effectively. *Be the Deal* convinced potential investors of the viability of ToExcel, and shortly after publication the company received $28 million in financing.

When I wrote *Be the Deal,* I was not concerned with the actual content of the book. I had a specific goal, which was to prove the concept of print on demand and help my cofounders of ToExcel achieve our investment goals to launch the company. However, I wanted to provide a useful book that would have integrity and interest for readers. The quickest book I could write to do that was my business biography, and that is what *Be the Deal* became.

Interestingly, in writing my business biography, I wrote in some places almost word for word the philosophy and concepts that Haanel had written almost a hundred years before. At first this may seem surprising, but when you analyze the true nature of wealth creation and the basic Law of Abundance and the other laws that Haanel, and now John and Richard, have written about in *Tapping the Source*, it is not surprising at all. Truth is truth, and effectiveness is effectiveness. Haanel had figured out the true keys to wealth and happiness. Fortunately for all of us, Richard brought this wisdom to my attention, and then through synchronicity I happened to be visiting Kauai, where John Selby lives, and John had the ideal writing and scientific background to bring the secret wisdom of Haanel to the widest possible audience. John's background as a cognitive psychologist was an extraordinary synchronicity. Richard and I could have found many other writers to help with the re-creation of the words in modern prose, but I truly believe only John had the necessary knowledge to in effect provide the "missing manual" for the actual exercises that Haanel mentioned but did not elaborate upon in his original text.

At first I was going to provide some additional insights and comments, as Richard has, but in rereading *Be the Deal*, I realized that even though it was written quickly and without editing, the concluding chapter, titled "Putting It All Together: The Seven-Step Program for Creating Your Own Good Luck in Business," closely follows the wisdom of Haanel. For those of you with a specific interest in manifesting money and abundance through business activities, these may be the final words for you to put into practice in your daily business activities.

Like Haanel, I believe that the universe contains unlimited abundance and that each and every human being has the capacity to fulfill every material, emotional, and creative desire just by connecting with or, as this book says, tapping the Source. The most important principle to creating true wealth is to be of service to others. Somehow I stumbled onto this truth at a very young age and in the process created a business, Waterside Productions, which has brought great happiness and wealth not only to me and my employees and clients and book publishers but also to the hundreds of millions of people who have read books "birthed" through my direct and indirect efforts. My work life has been an experience of pure joy, and the seven steps for creating luck, described on the following pages, are really the seven steps for tapping the Source and living a life of integrity and purpose. This is what I hope for each of you who reads these words. Of course, if you want to know more about the specific business techniques and experiences that led to these seven steps, *Be the Deal* is available to read in whole from iUniverse through Amazon and other book outlets.

Remember, these seven steps are complementary to the wisdom of Haanel that John and Richard share. They are my individual mantras for success, and I encourage you to formulate and share your own.

The Seven Steps to Creating Your Own Good Luck in Business

(Adapted and abridged from William Gladstone, *Be the Deal*, pages 137–141)

Step One: Aptitude

If you are going to create your own luck in business, it is absolutely essential that you have an aptitude for business and for deal making. This does not mean that you must be an instinctive deal maker, or that you were born thinking business, business, business. But at a minimum, you do need a basic aptitude for business and basic enjoyment of the rough-and-tumble nature of the business world. If you do not have this basic aptitude for business, you should probably not pursue business at all, as you are unlikely to be able to create your own luck or have any true enjoyment in your business life. This does not mean that you couldn't have a wonderful career as an artist, technician, teacher, or other professional for which you do have a basic aptitude and sense of enjoyment.

Step Two: Attitude

Once you have established that you have an aptitude for pursuing some aspect of the business world, you must develop a positive, can-do attitude. Part of your ability to create luck is your belief that you really are entitled to unlimited abundance and good fortune. You should cultivate this positive attitude by helping others and focusing on your accomplishments and personal gifts of health, energy, enthusiasm, and willingness to work toward your goals. By cultivating these qualities and acting as if you can take on any problem and contribute to any situation, you will start to see positive results in actually accomplishing these goals. Miraculously, you will begin to cultivate your own ability to be in the right place at the right time and to generally create your own luck.

Step Three: Application
Having a positive attitude and a basic aptitude for the specific area of work you have chosen will get you headed in the right direction, but you still must apply yourself. There is no substitute, particularly at the beginning of an endeavor or a career, for hard work. You need to be focused and ready when opportunity knocks, and you cannot be ready unless you are extremely well prepared in your field of specialization.

You need to know the vocabulary of your field and the basic structures and formulas that apply in your industry. You need to apply these principles whenever you can and learn from them so you know, almost intuitively, what is likely to work and what won't, at least based on industry standard experience. Just applying the principles of the past is never enough, but you can't begin to know when to deviate from the tried and true unless you understand the norms. You must know what the norms are, and, as in most pursuits, the deviations are not the norm by definition. Creating your own luck often will depend upon nothing more than observing trends and knowing what is likely to happen next.

I can't emphasize enough, however, the importance of applying yourself and obtaining a firm grounding in the fundamentals of your field. Picasso was an extremely accomplished realistic painter before he created modern techniques that defied the norms of his art. The same is true for innovators in other fields. Very rarely does it make good luck to step up to the plate not even knowing what kind of ball is going to be thrown at you, or without truly knowing the rules and logistics of the game.

Step Four: Acceptance

Accept yourself as you are, both your strengths and weaknesses of personality and character. You will be surprised to learn that no single attribute or quality you possess is ever in and of itself either a strength or weakness. There are always situations in which a quality that is normally a virtue can be a hindrance. Whether a quality is a strength or weakness for you depends upon the environment in which you are acting and the specific situation that presents itself to you.

Perhaps you are extremely bright and able to make quick decisions, and you believe that this is your greatest virtue. In most cases it probably is, but in instances in which your superiors do not want a quick decision made, you risk alienating an entire negotiation by coming up with too facile a solution. You may seem out of place or too ambitious and destroy an opportunity to succeed that a slower-thinking colleague would not risk.

In order to create your own luck, you must accept not only your own givens, but also the vagaries of the business world. You must be willing to accept risk and change and failure. Someone who never fails is not pushing the envelope far enough and will never reach their full potential. Good luck is less likely to visit the cautious than the brave, and it is only by accepting all that comes before you—even your own fears—that you can move into the space of courage, which will draw good luck to you.

Step Five: Awareness

Heightened self-awareness and awareness of your environment are essential to drawing any good luck to you, as is realizing that what I call magic is always in the air if you are ready for it and aware of its signs. Having an aptitude, cultivating a positive attitude, applying your skills and knowledge, and accepting yourself and your environment without resistance are keys to heightening your awareness.

Anyone who is fully aware can start to anticipate events and perfect his timing and strategize deals. Having the right energy and the right sense of timing automatically improves your odds of success and draws luck to you. There are a number of psychological techniques for increasing your awareness, but perhaps the easiest technique is to simply cultivate your breathing. Some people are born with greater capacity for awareness than others, but anyone can improve their awareness. It is partly a matter of courage. Don't stick your head in the sand and ignore potentially painful or embarrassing situations.

It is only by confronting situations head on, for good or bad, and looking clearly at the past, present, and probable future that you will be able to take advantage of silver linings in clouds and miraculously turn lemons into lemonade. Every situation has the potential for profit, or at least self-improvement. If you are aware of your own needs and those of others, you will see and feel the magic that others ignore. They will wonder at your good luck in surviving what on the surface might appear to be disastrous situations or even boneheaded mistakes. You will know that you created those lucky exits yourself.

Step Six: Abundance
Once you have experienced in a consistent pattern the five previous steps, you will begin to experience the feeling of abundance in your work life. This abundance will probably be manifested by greater earning capacity and a greater inflow of money to you. The key to abundance consciousness, however, is much more fundamental than having additional money. In my own life, having a lot of money in the bank was never as important as having the expectation of receiving a lot of money in the future. In practical terms, I would rather have $100,000 rolling in

a month with debts of $500,000 than $1 million in the bank, no debt, and no prospects for generating additional revenue. Since the guarantee of future revenues is always subject to some doubt, my abundance consciousness is really more dependent on my self-confidence and belief in my ability to generate future income than actual receivables. This abundance consciousness really can be learned and actually reflects the true nature of reality. There really are, on a universal basis, unlimited resources. You really can have everything you want on a material level, because there really is a finite limit to what material items you can desire, consume, or appreciate.

At a very basic level, money is merely energy, and the universe contains limitless energy. You need to cultivate an appreciation of the abundance of energy in the universe and your own role in cycling and recycling energy. Even if you have limited money at a particular moment in time, you have limitless enthusiasm, limitless joy, and limitless insights to share with others. By sharing your gifts with others, you restore your own personal store of energy and experience the truly abundant nature of the universe. Once you truly integrate this abundance consciousness, you will be even more open to the magical good fortune that is trying to reward you every day if you will only allow it to.

Step Seven: Appreciation

Even with a full implementation of the preceding six steps, you will not maximize the good luck in your life unless you also take time out to show and share your appreciation for the good fortune that is yours. Almost all successful entrepreneurs in the later stages of their development show their appreciation for the good fortune that society has bestowed upon them by giving back, whether it be by mentoring others or making billion-dollar gifts to the United Nations, like Ted Turner did. Even Bill Gates recognized that his main job now is giving away his fortune, through the Bill and Melinda Gates Foundation, not continuing to double or triple it every year.

But it is not enough to show your appreciation at the end of your life. You need to show it every day from the very beginning. You can show it in small ways, including private prayers of thanks, smiles to your employees, words of thanks to your colleagues, or sincere gratitude expressed to those who have helped you. There is no person among us who can succeed without a nurturing universe, and we should give thanks whenever possible. Good fortune smiles on those who appreciate their good fortune and who realize that their good fortune is not for their enjoyment alone, but for the betterment of the planet and of others. I would venture that anyone who has enjoyed good luck for any length of time, and even those who practice the six previous steps, would not long continue their string of good luck if they were not consciously appreciative and grateful to the universe for all that they have been given.

➤

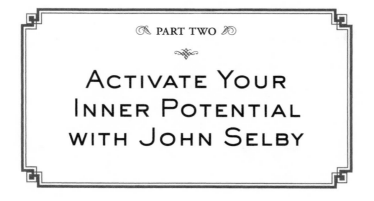

PART TWO

ACTIVATE YOUR INNER POTENTIAL WITH JOHN SELBY

❖ 6 ❖

REBIRTHING THE HAANEL VISION

※

harles Haanel never claimed to have invented the process of manifestation that he taught. In fact he often refers to classic sources in the Judeo-Christian heritage and Greek and Eastern traditions to highlight the ancient wisdom he's drawing from and expanding upon. But beyond classic parallels, his personal vision appears to be uniquely inspired with new psychological insights and remarkably clear elucidations of the core principles that drive our everyday lives:

> What you and I desire, what everyone is seeking, is happiness and harmony. If we can be truly happy, we shall have everything the world can give. If we are happy ourselves, we can make others happy.

One of the primary differentiating qualities of Haanel's vision is that he's not fixated on material possessions or giant bank accounts or a fleet of fancy cars in the garage. Yes, he does fully support abundance, but he bases his teachings on the fact that what we really want deep down is to feel genuinely happy and in ongoing harmony with ourselves and the world. As he says:

> Harmony and happiness are states of consciousness, and do not depend upon the possession of things.

After all the ongoing New Age media hype that has fixated over-much on manifesting material possessions and making money as one's primary intent, I was relieved to see Haanel stating the psychological and spiritual fact that the fulfillment we seek to manifest is ultimately an inner feeling, not an external situation.

It is our attitude of mind toward life which determines our experiences; if we expect nothing, we shall have nothing; if we demand much, we shall receive the greater portion.

Haanel was one of the first American writers to state core psychological facts that cognitive science would later "discover" in the 1960s and the New Age movement would fixate upon in the 1980s. Indeed, our chronic thoughts, attitudes, and beliefs do strongly and predictably determine what we manifest in life. Therefore, learning to consciously manage our thoughts and attitudes is the primary act in our search for fulfillment.

THE POWER TO MANIFEST

Creative power does not originate in the individual, but in the Universal, which is the source and foundation of all energy and substance; the individual is simply the channel for the distribution of this energy.

Here we find the foundation stone of Haanel's vision: that our personal manifestation power comes from a source beyond our individual ego identity. Furthermore:

The only real power which you can have is the power to adjust yourself to divine and unchangeable principles. You cannot change the Infinite, but you can come into an understanding of Natural laws.

Power does lie at the heart of Haanel's writings, because manifestation of any kind requires power. But his understanding of power extends considerably beyond our usual ego definitions of personal force. As this quote establishes, the natural laws of human manifestation are understood to function in harmony with the creative principles of the universe and beyond. Therefore, we gain individual power only to the extent that we adjust our thoughts and intent with universal laws. This is a giant difference from all the get-rich-quick manifestation programs claiming we can push our will upon the universe to get whatever we want. For Haanel, we must first adjust ourselves to universal principles if we are to access manifestation power.

The implications of this statement are profound, suggesting that in order to attain the deeper harmony and happiness we all desire, we must first access, understand, and adjust our personal attitudes and actions with the deeper reality of nature and the universe.

THE LAW OF ATTRACTION

One of the natural laws that imbues all of Haanel's writings and that will prove vital to this discussion is called the Law of Attraction. And right at the beginning, let's be clear on how Haanel equates the relationship among thought, attraction, and love:

> It is love which imparts vitality to thought and thus enables thought to germinate. The Law of Attraction, or the Law of Love, for they are one and the same, will bring to thought the necessary material for its growth and maturity.

Haanel historically was one of the first Americans to talk about the Law of Attraction—and in this book Richard, Bill, and I hope to clarify Haanel's expanded vision of how this underlying law operates. Notice, for instance, that in the above quote, love itself is the force that gives our thoughts their power to manifest. This essential integration of creative thought and harmonious feelings lies at the heart of Haanel's vision.

DESIRABLE THOUGHTS

Thought may lead to action of any kind, but whatever the action, it is simply the thought attempting to express itself in visible form. It is evident, therefore, that if we wish desirable conditions, we can afford to entertain only desirable thoughts.

The science of cognitive psychology has proven that our thoughts do carry the power to generate creative physical action. This is how something new comes into being in our lives. We first have a desire or passion for something (emotion), which leads to a creative thought (vision), which leads to physical action expressing that thought in visible form (manifestation).

Haanel was one of the first to clarify that if we want to increase desirable conditions in our lives (as we all do), then we must assume full responsibility for continually focusing our thoughts in desirable directions. As we'll see in this book, this is easier said than done, and a pragmatic daily method for maintaining desirable thoughts must be learned and applied.

Thought ordinarily leads outwardly in evolutionary directions, but it can be turned within, where it will take hold of the basic principles of things, the heart of things, the spirit of things. When you get to the heart of things it is comparatively easy to understand and command them.

Notice here that for Haanel, thought is a cognitive phenomenon that we can turn where we want to—and the key direction to turn our thoughts is "within" rather than "outwardly." For most people most of the time, thoughts run on autopilot, without conscious direction. Haanel's challenge is to take charge of your mind and aim your thoughts purposefully inward so that you "get to the heart of things."

Do you know how to do this? Do you do it often? Do you want to learn how to manage your thoughts more effectively? You might want to pause and reflect for a few moments on what we've talked about thus far, so that already in this program you take time to aim your attention inward, to your own source of inspiration.

REDEFINING ABUNDANCE

Haanel was definitely an advocate of abundance. He was a successful businessman in several large ventures, and he acknowledged that material possessions often help us to feel happy and fulfilled. He was also an advocate, as mentioned before, of becoming a person of power, explaining that in order to manifest, and to be of service to others, we must receive and expend power. But he put curious twists to the abundance theme, such as the following:

> Self-denial is not success. We cannot give unless we get; we cannot be helpful unless we are strong. If we wish to be of service to others we must have power—but to get it we must give it; we must be of service.

In the quote above, we find a primary law of manifestation and fulfillment—that power (and wealth itself) is not a static possession. It is an energetic charge that flows through our lives and equally the lives of those around us. This means that if we aren't busy giving and serving others, we won't receive power. It's that simple—yet far too often people focus on possessing power, not on sharing it.

Mind and Spirit

It's important to understand that Haanel often uses the words "Spirit" and "Mind" interchangeably in his teachings.

Spirit is Mind, because Spirit is intelligent.

Haanel was not, from my understanding, an esoteric man; he was in fact an early advocate of scientific examination, of logical deduction based on as much information as he could gather. But he constantly pushed beyond the known limits of science, in trying to understand the deeper ways in which the individual mind interacts with the Universal Mind.

At some point before he wrote *The Master Key System*, Haanel almost certainly had a revelatory spiritual experience, because his writings express a vision that transcends our normal logical boundaries and reveals a reality in which the intelligence, compassion, and creativity of one's individual mind arise from the intelligence, compassion, and creativity of the Infinite Mind that created and permeates the universe.

Reflecting this expanded understanding, in which our material universe continually emerges from a higher creative source, he wrote:

The essence and soul of all things is spiritual; the spiritual is the real, because it is the life of all there is; when the spirit is gone, the life is gone.

Haanel strongly differentiated between "spiritual" and "religious." For him, "religious" referred to a cognitive set of belief systems created by the human mind based on past history and future projection, whereas "spiritual" referred to the direct present-moment experience of one's creative communion with the Infinite Divine.

Haanel insisted that he didn't want any new religion to emerge based on his spiritual and psychological insights (even so, several religions, notably the Church of Religious Science, did come into being based on his teachings). Instead, he aimed attention away from external theologies, beliefs, and social institutions and toward a regular shift of attention inward to one's Source, where direct encounter with the Divine is experienced:

> The great fact is that the source of all life and all power is found within. This means that the insight, strength and power to answer our needs will be found within.

Many New Age manifestation programs are focused outward on what people think will bring them happiness—more money, lovers, stocks and bonds, physical health, tropical getaways, and so on. Haanel refreshingly insists that we must learn how to focus within, toward the true source of our power, in order to manifest.

Unfortunately, most people have a deucedly difficult time shifting their focus away from external things, toward their internal universal core of power and being. This is where I hope to add process to Haanel's vision. Specifically I would like to teach you how to employ a set of newly developed Focus Phrases, inspired by Haanel's teachings, that will help quiet your thoughts and aim your focus of attention inward—to where your power and happiness are awaiting your attention.

THE POWER OF GIVING

> The more we give, the more we shall get; we must become a channel whereby the Universal can express activity. The Universal is constantly seeking to express itself, to be of service, and it seeks the channel whereby it can find the greatest activity, where it can do the most good.

The entire universe for Haanel is a magnificent infinite creative flow of intelligent harmonious energy; in this regard his vision closely matches that of Einstein, who was his contemporary. When Einstein stated that "the intent of the experimenter influences the outcome of the experiment," he was expressing a core element of Haanel's manifestation methodology: that "everything influences everything."

> Every transaction must benefit every person in any way connected with the transaction—because the individual is a part of the Universal. The welfare of each part depends upon a recognition of the interest of the whole.

To be honest, far too much of the New Age movement has been focused on selfish intent. But for Haanel, "the interest of the whole" must permeate our thoughts about manifestation, not because of any moralistic dogma, but because that's simply how the universe operates.

UNIVERSAL MIND

> The Universal Mind is the totality of all mind in existence. The universe must have been thought into shape, before it could become a material fact. And we find our thoughts taking form, just as the universe took form. It is the same mind, operating through the individual.

Throughout his writings, Haanel makes clear that the inflow of what he calls Spirit or Universal Wisdom or Infinite Intelligence and other names is the true source of our power and inspiration, connecting our individual consciousness with the Architect of the Universe.

By the way, if it helps you to think the word "God" when Haanel says "Universal Mind" or "Creative Source" or whatever, please feel free. Terms such as "Allah," "Tao," "Yahweh," the "Naguah'l," and so forth found throughout our world cultures are all labels for the one infinite, compassionate creator of our universe and beyond. All words can do is point our attention toward shared experiences. That's communication—and Haanel used carefully selected words that resonate deeply with common human experience and expanded spiritual realization.

AFFIRMATIONS AND FOCUS PHRASES

Haanel is considered one of the originators of affirmations. But note the difference between his affirmations and most of the affirmations that are popular today.

> The affirmation "I am whole, perfect, strong, powerful, loving, harmonious, and happy" will bring about harmonious conditions. The reason for this is because the affirmation is in strict accordance with the Truth, and when Truth appears every form of error or discord must necessarily disappear.

As I discovered on my own a couple of decades ago, and as Haanel clearly shows here, affirmations have no power if they are not grounded in reality, in "Truth," as he calls it. To possess power, they must be "in strict accordance" with natural laws, with unselfish desires, with the higher good.

The Focus Phrases that I'll be teaching you throughout this book, in the last section of each chapter, are based on this employment of carefully worded, reality-based sentences used as mental tools to point your attention in directions that connect you with the Universal Mind, by whatever name. In so doing, these Focus Phrases will help bring you into resonance with the natural laws that sustain your life and nurture your goals.

> "I am whole, perfect, strong, powerful, loving, harmonious, and happy."

Does this statement reflect your own deeper potential? From Haanel's perspective, it is indeed true that we are right now "perfect" beings—because God's entire creation is perfect and we are an expression of that perfection once we put aside self-judgment. Likewise we are "whole" when we allow ourselves to realize our true oneness with our Creator. We're certainly "strong" and "powerful" when we reconnect with our infinite power source. We're "loving" when we learn to focus our attention habitually in positive compassionate directions. And we're "harmonious" and "happy" when we master the fine art of holding our focus inward to our true infinite unity with the Universal Mind.

Similar to Jesus saying, "Be ye therefore perfect, even as your Father in heaven is perfect," Haanel insists that you and I are already perfect whole empowered beings—except for our negative judgmental thoughts that separate us from our true infinite nature. If we learn to successfully manage our thoughts and focus regularly toward connecting with our true nature, we are in fact one with our Creator—not sometime in the future, once we improve ourselves, but right now.

Well-crafted affirmations and Focus Phrases are mental tools for redirecting attention in successful directions. My rule in generating Focus Phrases is that they must aim our attention in directions that we all naturally desire but too often forget. They must resonate with the higher laws and aim toward the higher good. And they must be powerful in eliciting an immediate inner response.

Because the thoughts you hold in your mind determine what happens in your life, it's vital to assume conscious responsibility for your thoughts. This is the basic logic of Haanel's teachings. When you've finished reading this book, you'll have learned a set of Focus Phrases that will be of primary assistance in managing your mind to your higher advantage.

PASSION AND WORK

A thought's vitality depends upon the feeling with which the thought is impregnated. If the thought is passionate and constructive, it will possess vitality; it will have life; it will grow, develop, expand; it will be creative; it will attract to itself everything necessary for its complete development.

This quote expresses a major aspect of Haanel's manifestation process, and indeed of his deeper philosophy of life: that thought without feeling is nothing. An idea without passion is powerless. Desire and yearning are the driving force of an idea, and without them no idea will achieve success.

In fact, for Haanel, the passion must come first, then the thought. First you identify what you hunger for, what you are yearning to achieve or experience or own, and if this passion resonates with your higher Mind and the natural laws of the universe, inspired thoughts will come flowing into your mind with creative ideas and insights into how to manifest your yearning and passion in the physical domain.

Every success has been accomplished by persistent concentration upon the object in view.

Again from Haanel there comes a primal challenge: In order to manifest what you desire in life, you must make a persistent effort to focus your attention directly toward what you want. Work will still be required, following the vision. You must continue to hold your mind's awareness toward your ultimate goal.

Accomplishing this focusing goal can prove difficult without the proper mental tools. This is where most of us encounter what we consider failure in achieving our goals. We tend to lack discipline and focus. Therefore, I'll be teaching you the most effective focusing methods so far devised, based on the integration of ancient meditative techniques and potent new insights from cognitive psychology.

Your Solar Plexus

Over and over again, Haanel returns to the question—where does this Universal Wisdom by whatever name actually enter into our personal bodies and awareness? His answer surprised and enlightened me: He insists that insights and empowerment from our Universal Source flow into human consciousness not directly to the brain, or the heart, but rather through the solar plexus—that energetic center of our organism where heartbeat and breathing function in intimate harmony to maintain personal vitality and creativity.

> The solar plexus is the point at which the part meets with the whole, where the Infinite becomes finite, Universal becomes individualized, Invisible becomes visible. It's the point at which life appears, and there is no limit to the amount of life you can generate from this solar center.

Having focused for many years mostly on my heart center as the locus of spiritual and energetic inflow, I found this statement challenging. We usually think of inspired insight flowing into our brains, or perhaps into our hearts. In this book I'd like to explore with you this dictum, by teaching you an "open to receive" meditation that might truly change your life.

Mental Attitudes

In the mid-1960s at the University of Pennsylvania, a psychology professor named Aaron Beck formally launched a new division of experimental enquiry called cognitive science, in which the attitudes and beliefs we inherit as children and advance as adults are the determining dynamic in all that we accomplish in life.

There is actually very little to be found at the core of cognitive psychology and its highly successful offspring, cognitive therapy, that Haanel didn't clarify fifty years earlier. Indeed, ancient yogic masters such as Patanjali in ancient India very clearly laid out the same insights: that our attitudes determine our thoughts, our thoughts stimulate emotions, and our emotions motivate actions that determine what happens in our lives.

Haanel taught that by aligning our personal attitudes with the natural laws of the universe, and by opening to receive insights that further advance our attitudes in successful directions, we can transform our lives in positive ways and attract the material environment that we desire to make us feel happy and harmonious:

> If we desire material possession of any kind, our chief concern should be to acquire the mental attitude which will bring about the result desired. This mental attitude is brought about by a realization of our spiritual nature and our unity with the Universal Mind, which is the substance of all things. This realization will bring about everything which is necessary for our complete enjoyment.

Within the scope of this book you will be encouraged to take a concerted look at your existing mental attitudes. You will discover which ones serve you and which ones hold you back—and, as Haanel encourages, throw out the ones that hold you back. You're also going to learn to master the process of cognitive shifting, in which you actively redirect your attention toward attitudes that powerfully serve you.

SILENCE

Over and over, Haanel points our attention inward to experience a state of consciousness he calls the Silence:

It is in Silence that you get in touch with the omnipotent power of the subconscious mind from which all power is evolved. Intuition usually comes in the Silence; great minds seek solitude frequently. Silence is the condition required for all great purposes.

Throughout all meditative traditions, learning how to enter regularly into inner silence has been a primary tool. Why? Because quieting the mind does predictably lead to contact with the Divine. In the Old Testament, for instance, we find the remarkable contemplative challenge: "Be still, and know that I am God."

The human mind tends to generate a nonstop habitual stream of consciousness that dominates one's focus with seemingly random thoughts and images, memories and imaginations, worries and daydreams. Only when we learn to quiet the nonstop chatter of our ego minds can we begin to listen to the deeper voice that speaks to us beyond our mental chatter. That inner voice comes to us quite effortlessly in the midst of moments of silence, when we suddenly know our true spiritual nature directly. And as Haanel points out, from this inner infinite knowingness emerge all of our sudden flashes of insight that in turn point us toward creativity, harmony, manifestation, and happiness.

The Process

Whether you desire a new love mate or a new job, better health or a better backhand, higher grade scores or higher spiritual harmony, and regardless of the type of manifestation, big or small, that you seek in life, here's the pragmatic procedure that I've found most effective.

First you need to learn a method to temporarily silence the nonstop mental chatter that usually runs through the back of your mind with all sorts of chronic fixations and worries. There are new cognitive methods that enable you to quickly quiet your thoughts.

Once you quiet your ego's nonstop monologue, you enter into the Silence and begin to open up and listen to your deeper inner voice, to realize what you need in your life to feel happy, healthy, and in harmony. Tune in, be honest with yourself, and experience insight.

Here's how Haanel expresses this power of entering into the Silence where we can "truly think":

> For the realization of conscious power, we should seek the Silence frequently. Power comes through repose; it is in the Silence that we can be still, and when we are still, we can truly think, and thought is the secret of all attainment.

And once you become clear as to what you truly desire to manifest, then you will need to bring your focus of intent regularly to your goal, day in and day out, so that you channel power and insight, strategy and action, in directions that manifest your dream.

Logically, based on the insights that Haanel puts forth and that have inspired this book, there exists a natural psychological process that you can identify, explore, master, and apply often to maximize your effectiveness in life. Here's the seven-step procedure that we'll be learning in this book:

1. Remember to pause and turn inward.

2. Quiet your mind and enter into the Silence.

3. Open inwardly to receive insight from your Source.

4. Identify a primary need or desire you want to fulfill.

5. Through focusing on your solar plexus, connect with the infinite manifestation power of the Universal Mind.

6. Focus devotedly upon your vision and your goal.

7. Continue to employ the "power of attraction" process so that you act step by step to manifest your dream.

This is the core manifestation session that we will encourage you to master and move through each new day, so that you stay tuned into your connection with the Universal Manifestation Force.

As mentioned before, you can do several of these manifestation sessions each day, to meet your various needs. You can also pause for a couple of minutes, perhaps three to six times a day, to refocus upon an inner manifestation intent, so that your mind continues to nurture the manifestation process as your life progresses. That's the full daily routine that will generate the results you want.

We heartily welcome you to this exploration and awakening of your personal potential to tap your inner source of creation, harmony, and happiness. By looking to the core of your needs and desires, and then actively focusing on manifesting the harmony, abundance, love, and fulfillment that you hunger for and fully deserve, you'll achieve the life mastery that Haanel so lucidly encourages.

As a gentle beginning step in the direction of acting to fulfill your current and long-term needs, large or small, see what you experience in the next moments if you put this book aside. Tune into your breathing for a few relaxed inhales and exhales, and then see what comes effortlessly to mind as you ask yourself the following questions: What is it that I really want to bring into my life? How do I want to change or advance my current situation so as to make me feel truly happy and fulfilled?

❖ 7 ❖

UNIVERSAL CREATIVE MIND

~≈≈~

This is a reality-based book about your manifestation powers and how you can learn to activate, manage, and express those powers at a higher level. You don't need to "believe" anything in order for this program to work for you—all you need to do is open yourself to actual experience and discover for yourself the results of the process.

At the heart of this program is the understanding that there exists a Universal Manifestation Power, a pervading nonphysical consciousness, that willingly and in fact eagerly chooses to flow in when invited into our personal consciousness.

> The Universal Mind is the intelligence which pervades all space and animates all living things. The ability of the individual to think is his ability to act upon the Universal Mind and convert it into dynamic mind, or mind in motion.

What is the nature of this Universal Mind, and how does Haanel's vision of our Creator fit into our culture's existing spiritual, philosophical, and scientific understandings of the nature of the universe and beyond?

I remember a sunny springtime morning about twenty-five years ago, when I was sitting in the dining car of the Vienna-Berlin express, sipping a strong coffee, and flipping through the pages of a *Scientific American* magazine I'd bought at the train station. I became quickly engrossed in a discussion of string theory and several other new scientific visions of the universe that daring members of the "new physics" were proposing. What struck me especially strongly was the emerging theory that there simply must be more than four dimensions to the universe in order to explain new discoveries in physics.

Somehow, reading that statement in a revered scientific journal made me sigh with relief—finally science and religion seemed to be coming to the same conclusions about the nature of the universe. As I stared out the train's window at the onion-shaped spires of Austria's traditional churches, I reflected upon Christian beliefs based on the existence of dimensions entirely beyond the space-time continuum—in the realms of nonphysical transpersonal Spirit.

I also found myself remembering the inspired words of a Buddhist spiritual teacher from Burma back in the late 1960s in San Francisco. Thakin Kung had likewise insisted, from his deep meditation experience, that there exist without question numerous "consciousness dimensions" beyond the scientific dimensions of physical volume and chronological time.

Thakin taught that consciousness itself, the very thoughts that run through our minds and the imaginations that spring into being inside our heads, exist in a dimension outside of the space-time continuum, in a fifth dimension within which we spend our entire lives, like fish in water, without even noticing.

Haanel also posits a fifth dimension of consciousness that we all live within and are sustained by. This dimension is the intelligent energetic glue that holds together the space-time continuum, and through it the transcendent power of intuitive thought can flow into our personal bubbles of awareness and thus influence our physical world. Haanel often calls this fifth dimension the Universal Mind:

> The Universal Mind is not only Intelligence, it is substance, and this substance is the attractive force which brings electrons together by the Law of Attraction so that they form atoms; the atoms in turn are

brought together by the same law and form molecules. This Law of Attraction, which is also the Law of Love, is the creative force behind every manifestation—not only of atoms but of worlds, of the Universe, of everything of which the imagination can form any conception.

For Haanel, this entire physical universe is made up of Universal Mind, and that's why we can employ the power of consciousness to manifest what we desire in life. As we saw before, Haanel believes (along with the ancient Hindu masters and many other spiritual teachers) that before the creation of our physical universe there existed a primordial power and Consciousness utterly beyond the imagination of our mortal minds. And this Universal Mind somehow simply "thought" our material universe into being during the nanosecond of the Big Bang.

The creation equation is clear for Haanel: First came the desire (passion). Then came the thought (imagination). Then came the physical expression (manifestation).

I remember as a child reading and rereading one particular sentence in the New Testament's Gospel according to John: "In the beginning was the Word, and the Word was with God, and the Word was God." So we find in the Judeo-Christian tradition the exact same creative vision that drives Haanel's manifestation process. "The Word" is another term for Thought. Thought was present before and at the beginning of our universe. Thought is the Creative Force ("and the Word was God").

In case you missed the following primary Haanel quote I offered in the previous chapter, here's his creation dictum:

The universe must have been thought into shape, before it could become a material fact.

Haanel is with this quote doing the one thing that materialist scientists cannot: He's looking back to before the Big Bang creation event and describing how the Big Bang was actually generated—by the power of thought emerging from the Universal Creative Mind. There pre-existed an infinite intelligence, a vast power, a loving being, that through thought brought our universe into mind, and thought the universe into existence.

Here's the key point that animates this book: That same pre-existing infinite dimension that created our material universe (the dimension of infinite creative thought) continues to permeate our universe and to animate and instruct and inspire our own creative thoughts. And our individual thoughts, when inspired by the Universal Mind, are a chip off the old block in that they also hold unlimited power to create:

> The unlimited creative power of the Universal Mind is within control of the conscious mind of the individual. We can have the inspiration of the omnipotent Universal Mind on demand at any time.

Haanel was adamant that each of us is a perfect expression of our Creator, and that we can tap into our Creator's power at will. Of course, Jesus himself spoke heretically when he said, "This which I do, and even more, you can also do."

It is this direct link between our Creator and our own creative minds that lies at the heart of Haanel's teachings and the manifestation method being taught in this book. This is why we're beginning our discussion focused upon the Universal Creative Mind—because if you habitually deny your own ability to tap the power of your Creator, you in essence don't have that power. You must recognize your higher nature and regularly turn your attention directly toward this inner Source of infinite creation if you want to access creative vision and manifest your higher desires.

There are always limitations blocking our success when we fixate upon these limitations. Haanel instead insists that we discipline our minds to focus upon our infinite oneness with the Universal Mind, so that we break free from limitations:

The Universal Mind is unconditional; therefore the more conscious we become of our unity with this Mind, the less conscious we shall become of conditions and limitations, and as we become emancipated or freed from conditions, we come into a realization of the unconditional. We have become free!

This is a massive statement, one to be pondered deeply until it becomes lucid in our minds. Haanel is welcoming us emphatically to move in the direction of being conscious of the fact that, even right now, we are not separate from the infinite creative force of the universe. Indeed, we are in an active state of "unity with this Mind."

You must of course decide for yourself what you think about all this. As we'll see in chapters to come, Haanel doesn't insist that you believe his vision; he insists that you learn how to enter into the Silence, quiet your mind, and discover for yourself as a direct experience the reality of what he's describing. And I entirely agree.

Don't continue to generate new and bigger beliefs based on what you hope might be true. Instead quiet all your ego imaginations, look honestly at what's real, focus within to your Source, experience what's true, and, as Haanel encourages, surrender and align your beliefs with the truth, and throw out any fantasy, no matter how sacred, that is not in perfect resonance with God's creation, with the Universal Mind itself. This is the path to power.

The Universal Mind is the live wire. It carries power sufficient to meet every situation which may arise in the life of every individual. When the individual mind touches the Universal Mind it receives all the power it requires. This happens in the world within.

Our challenge is to make sure that, on a regular basis, our "individual mind touches the Universal Mind." We must somehow remember to remember that we are more than the mental and emotional programmings that we inherited from our parents and our community and culture. It's so easy to slip back into relative unconsciousness, and a major part of this book and process is the development of new habits that help us remember that we are in constant control of where we choose to focus our attention. And everything in our life is determined by where we focus our attention, moment to moment.

To begin the pragmatic part of this book, let's explore the power of just one carefully tuned Focus Phrase that almost instantly re-aims your attention exactly where Haanel recommends aiming it: toward your own inner center of being, where you in fact encounter the Source that will empower this entire process of manifestation.

If you can remember to regularly refocus your attention inward in a joyful spirit, you'll regain that essential mental posture that in turn will enable you to advance through the full manifestation process.

Step 1: Remember to Remember

Always the first step in a daily manifestation program is remembering to pause and move through the program. If you don't remember to pause, you'll probably continue to run on autopilot and not make progress. So it's time to introduce the first step of practical action that you can take, inside your own heart and mind, to shift your attitudes and inner experience in directions that will promote active manifestation of your dream.

What's the first step to manifestation? To regain a positive emotion in the process of aiming your attention directly inward, toward the experience of Universal Mind deep within your consciousness.

One of Haanel's assumptions is that turning your attention toward God, toward the Universal Mind, does make you feel better, in and of itself. As we've already seen, he also insists that if you don't feel good inside your own skin, you're not going to manifest a good-feeling dream. Let's take another look at what we quoted Haanel saying earlier:

What you and I desire, what everyone is seeking, is happiness and
harmony. If we can be truly happy, we shall have everything the
world can give.

Do you agree with this statement?

The word "happiness" has become as overused as the word "love" in
our society, to the point where we've perhaps lost touch with the power of
the term. I hope that you rediscover the term's power in this book, because
it's vital to openly admit to our core intent of somehow learning to feel
happy, rather than unhappy, in daily life.

It's the same with the term "inner harmony." For Haanel, this quality
is the foundation of happiness and success in life:

Harmony in the world within will be reflected in the world without
by harmonious conditions, by agreeable surroundings, and the best
of everything. Inner harmony is the foundation of health and a necessary essential to all greatness, all power, all attainment, all achievement, and all success.

To manifest more harmony and happiness in your life,
Haanel urges you to regularly return your attention toward positive
thoughts and harmonious emotions. Focus on what you want
to manifest—that's the primary act! But often it seems impossible
to even attempt to do this because there's so much negative stuff in
one's life.

Haanel doesn't deny the negative. He simply recommends that
you turn your attention regularly away from all the negative stuff and
choose to focus on what you want to manifest, which ultimately is
feeling good and in harmony, and enjoying each new moment—which
ultimately means feeling tuned in to your inner source of life and love
and good feelings.

Okay, here's the Focus Phrase that will instantly help you shift your focus toward the ultimate source of feeling better:

"I choose to focus enjoyably inward."

There you have it—the statement of intent that in turn generates the ultimate refocusing of attention. Your challenge is to silently say this clear, powerful statement of intent regularly to yourself, so that you hold this key focus in your mind and heart as you go about your day.

Say it. Do it! Choose to focus enjoyably inward. And make this choice often during each new day.

MASTERING THE FIRST STEP

Let's examine this core statement more closely. Notice first of all that by saying this Focus Phrase, you are clarifying that there is a choice to be made—and you're making it right now.

"I choose . . ." And what are you choosing? To focus inward to make contact with your infinite wellspring of harmony and joy— toward pleasure rather than pain, brightness over darkness, joy instead of depression. Each moment, there is this decision: what to focus on. And you are exercising your power to choose positive over negative, and to focus on inner spiritual experience rather than external mundane fixations.

Almost everyone wants to feel good, not bad. Given the choice, you want to experience creativity and harmony, not stagnation and conflict. Furthermore, almost everyone prefers to be in tune with their spiritual core of being, rather than feeling disconnected.

What you're doing with this first Focus Phrase is shifting from being passive to being active in determining your inner condition. You're making a choice, and acting on it!

How does such a seemingly simple statement of positive intent generate action? It's cognitive science 101:

When your guiding ego voice states its intent, the rest of your being immediately responds.

In this case, you focus your attention inward, toward the ultimate fountain of happiness, and in so doing you stop fixating on all the external things that might make you feel bad.

Each new moment, it's your choice to decide whether you're going to enjoy this moment or remain stuck in thoughts and fixations that dampen your spirit and weaken your power to manifest what you want.

As mentioned earlier, one of Haanel's driving points concerning the human dilemma is that you're continually choosing where you're going to focus your all-powerful attention—on negative or positive thoughts. When you run mostly on habit and instinct, you remain a victim of habitual mood swings, of external events, of the ups and downs at work, or of your lover's whims.

Only when you act so as to be more conscious can you choose where to focus your mind's attention and thus choose your own moods.

Look at this a bit more closely. At any given moment, there are usually a dozen things present in your mind, emotions, or environment that, if you focus on them, will make you feel bad. You might have an ache or pain somewhere physically that you can fixate on and suffer. You can remember something terrible that happened to you in the past, relive the terrible event, and feel horrible. You can worry about something that might happen in the future and generate any sort of negative feeling. That's your choice.

Likewise there are almost always quite a great number of things to focus on that will immediately boost your mood and make you feel happy. Right now you can remember something enjoyable from the past, you can imagine something beautiful in the future, you can tune into where you feel especially good in your body, or you can focus on any number of positive sensory or social or intimate experiences around you, and thus bring happy feelings into your life.

But the source of all good feelings is found beyond sensations, beyond bright ideas and feelings about your external life, and in this first Focus Phrase, "I choose to focus enjoyably inward," you're instantly aiming your attention where you know you'll find good feelings.

Whatever else you're doing each moment, you can remain tuned into your inner source of happiness and harmony.

Therefore I strongly encourage you to develop a new habit: holding this potent beginning Focus Phrase in your mind as much as you can, regardless of what you're doing, and letting it effortlessly aim your attention toward feeling bright, empowered, and inspired by your inner infinite Source.

This is how you can predictably optimize happiness and positive manifestation in your life. The statement leads directly to a response throughout your being.

And yes, practice does make perfect. Perhaps you'll feel very little in the way of positive mood uplift the first few times you say this elicitor statement, but continue to memorize and master the inner process for a few days and you'll develop a fond addiction to holding this statement of positive intent in the back of your mind as you move through each new day.

This Focus Phrase will become your lifeline for breaking out of old negative mood habits and passing through Haanel's "joy portal" into a transforming life experience—over and over again!

Right now, if you want, I encourage you to take a breather from reading and shift into experiencing. Say the Focus Phrase again silently to yourself as you exhale, and then as you inhale be open to a new experience:

"I choose to focus enjoyably inward."

❖ 8 ❖

ENTERING INTO CREATIVE SILENCE

❦

We saw clearly in the last chapter that the path to successful manifestation and joy in life is to focus toward the inner source of that joy and success. As Haanel puts it:

When the individual mind touches the Universal Mind, it receives all the power it requires to manifest. This happens in the world within.

In order to understand the process through which your individual mind can touch the Universal Mind, let's see what Haanel means by the individual mind. Then I'll teach you a pragmatic method for bringing your individual mind predictably in touch with the Universal Mind.

Manifestation is often considered an individual act of conscious willpower. We decide that we want to have something that we don't have or that perhaps doesn't even exist yet in our physical world. We choose to set our intent on acting to obtain this thing or situation or experience. We purposefully develop a strategy for how to manifest what we want and then go into action by using our intelligence and willpower to push ahead and do what must be done in order to achieve our goal.

When we perceive ourselves as isolated intelligent physical bodies driven by selfish egos, we limit our power of achievement to our biological potential, rather than our higher potential. There's nothing wrong with this, but indeed it does limit us considerably and inhibit the deeper feeling of fulfillment that we seek. Here's how Haanel says this:

The fundamental principle of creative power is in the Universal, and therefore the idea of forcing an action by the power of the individual will is an inverted conception, which may appear to succeed for a while but is eventually doomed to failure—because it antagonizes the very power which it is seeking to use.

We have enough individual ego power to force a certain level of manifestation to happen. But Haanel continually insists that our personal will must be in harmony with the Greater Will if we are to not only grab what we want in life, but also come into possession of those things and situations and relationships that truly nurture deep satisfaction. And this higher path to fulfillment involves coordination of two quite different functions of the mind, so that our personal willpower and intellectual reasoning work together with the "higher" functions of the mind that are plugged into the Universal Mind and its infinite manifestation powers.

Reflecting the new psychological terminologies of his historic period, in which Sigmund Freud and Carl Jung were actively leading a revolution in human thinking, Haanel often used the terms "conscious" versus "subconscious," or "objective" versus "subjective," to differentiate two different vital functions of the human mind: our two "centers of our being," as he called them.

It is the coordination of these two centers of our being, and the understanding of their functions, which is the great secret of life. With this knowledge we can bring the objective and subjective minds into conscious cooperation and thus coordinate the finite and the infinite.

Our conscious mind is the perceptual observing mind of the senses, plus all the cognitive symbols and thoughts that emerge based on past experiences and rational reflection. We have an experience, respond to that experience, reflect upon it, categorize it, and perhaps change our ideas about life based on the experience. We also use past experience to fantasize and think up plans for the future—and decide how to act so as to manifest our creative projections.

The outward and changeable function has been termed the conscious mind, which deals with outward objects. Perceiving and operating through the five physical senses, the conscious mind deals with the impressions and objects of the outward life. It has the faculty of discrimination, carrying with it the responsibility of choice. It has the power of reasoning. It is the seat of the will.

Often people tend to think that this reasoning, willful, strategy-prone function of the mind is the primary driver of our manifestation powers. But for Haanel, the conscious mind comes into power only when it temporarily becomes quiet and surrenders to the other primary function of the mind, which he calls subjective, unconscious, intuitive, creative, and spiritual.

We are related to the world within by the subconscious mind, which includes all subjective sensations such as joy, fear, love, emotion, respiration, imagination, insight, and wisdom. It is through the subconscious that we are connected with the Universal Mind and brought into relation with the infinite constructive forces of the universe.

This is a very strong statement from Haanel, and once again he's doing his best to employ words and concepts to speak of the ineffable dimensions of reality that lie beyond our senses, that transcend the conscious mind's rational vistas and limitations. And once again, I don't expect you to just nod your head and agree with these words. Rather, I hope to lead you through an experiential process that will let you find out for yourself what lies beyond these words.

Scientists remain mostly baffled by the phenomenon of intuition, by the creative flashes of insight and spiritual realization that all humans are prone to. Cognitive psychology has ascertained that the left side of the brain is associated with deductive conscious logic and reason, as well as perception and willful intent, and that the right side of the brain is mostly devoted to creativity, insight, and subjective feelings.

And at times, both sides seem to fire off together, in what some neurologists refer to as the "integrative function of the mind." But this is a mere label, aiming our attention toward a high-mind phenomenon that science cannot quite grasp. Why? Because right at the point where the conscious rational mind interacts with the unconscious intuitive mind, as we've seen, the traditional space-time material model of reality seems to expand into dimensions that science cannot as yet demonstrate.

So we have this universally shared understanding that our individual conscious minds do sometimes come into active contact with important but subtle realms of realization and empowerment, through the subconscious mind, and that if we properly manage our minds, through this interaction of personal and universal we can predictably tap into the manifestation power of our Creator.

> The subconscious mind perceives by intuition, and its processes are rapid. Those who trust the subconscious find that they have infinite resources at their command.

That said, what is the relationship between the conscious and the unconscious mind in the manifestation process? First we must learn, as stated before, how to quiet the chatter of the conscious mind long enough to tune into our unconscious needs and desires, and to link ourselves with the Universal Mind's wisdom and power. That accomplished, we can then use the conscious mind's special power to focus on our goals and to will our manifestation desires to happen step by step in our lives.

When the conscious mind states to the subconscious mind specific things to be accomplished, forces are set in operation that lead to the result desired. Herein lies the power of the conscious mind: The subconscious can and will carry out such plans and ideas as may be suggested to it by the conscious mind.

Over and over, we're going to keep returning to this basic manifestation process, discovering step by step how to actually do what we're talking about. Let's pause a moment and reflect.

Do you agree with this basic understanding of who you are and how you can learn to manage your mind so as to achieve your higher goals?

Perhaps you might want to take a bit of time to put the book aside, and reflect upon your own feelings concerning your personal relationship with the Infinite Mind.

Does this discussion ring true for you? In your personal experience, are Haanel's lofty ideas just words on paper, or have you discovered in your own life that you are in fact more than just a physical brain and body?

Right now do you feel connected with an infinite Creative Source that brought this entire physical universe into existence? Or are you nothing more than an isolated bubble of awareness with no connection to a greater manifestation power?

Pause . . . and reflect.

Quiet Your Mind and Tap Your Source

A key premise Haanel teaches is that you must learn how to regularly quiet the usual habitual thoughts in your mind, that stream of consciousness that chatters nonstop and occupies so much of your attention. Why stop this chatter? Because only in the midst of inner silence can you shift fully into the intuitive "unconscious" state of mind in which you connect with, listen to, and receive from the Universal Mind.

Stated succinctly:

It is in the Silence that you will get into touch with the omnipotent power of the subconscious mind from which all power is evolved.

In all the world's meditative and contemplative traditions, this same basic notion is taught: that we must somehow quiet our minds and enter into the Silence if we want to tap into the infinite realms of consciousness that lie beyond the limited everyday realms of our senses and biological brains.

Intuition usually comes in the Silence; great minds seek solitude frequently; it is here that all the larger problems of life are worked out. For this reason every businessman who can afford it has a private office, where he will not be disturbed; if you cannot afford a private office you can at least find somewhere where you can be alone a few minutes each day and enter into Silence, which will enable you to develop that invincible power which you yearn to achieve.

One of the reasons I'm writing this book is because Haanel speaks so strongly about the requirement of regularly quieting the mind, but offers no concrete guidelines or methods for achieving this initial manifestation goal. He makes the following beginning statement, from which we will expand:

The Silence is necessary, the senses must be stilled, the muscles relaxed, repose cultivated. When you come into possession of a sense of poise and power you will be ready to receive the information or inspiration or wisdom necessary for the development of your purpose.

Back in the late 1960s I was lucky enough to be at the right place at the right time to participate in seminal research exploring the underlying "quiet-mind" psychological process common to all the world's meditative traditions. New research has amplified these early discoveries. I'd like to share with you the formal quiet-mind process we've now developed, devoid of traditional theological and esoteric trappings, for quickly entering into the Silence.

Psychologically, most of us most of the time are caught up in nonstop thoughts and imaginings that pull our attention away from the present moment, into past and future fixations. We can continue with our mental ruminations and be aware of one present-moment sensory event at the same time.

But as soon as we focus our attention on two or more sensory events at the same time, all of our habitual thoughts temporarily stop.

It's that simple—and almost all meditative techniques from antiquity designed to quiet the mind's chatter have been based on this universal psychological fact.

Through combining old-time meditation techniques with current psychological insights, we've recently created a core method for quieting your mind and entering into the Silence whenever you so choose. This quiet mind is the primary foundation you will require in order to succeed in consciously creating the life that you desire.

STEP 2: QUIET YOUR MIND

As you learned in the previous chapter, the initial step (and the intent of the first Focus Phrase) in this method is always to pause and give yourself permission to feel good. Remember to say to yourself, "I choose to enjoy this moment."

The next step is also seemingly simple yet deeply profound: looking inward and actively turning your mind's focus of attention directly and with full concentration toward a core sensation that's happening all the time whether you're aware of it or not, the sensation of the air flowing in and out of your nose each new moment.

Even as you read these words, you can right now become aware of the air flowing in and out of your nose, not as an idea but as an actual sensation. Feel it!

Whenever you want to, you can use your thinking mind to direct your attention exactly where you want it by saying to yourself the following Focus Phrase:

"I feel the air flowing in and out of my nose."

Notice the careful selection of words here. Usually in a traditional breath meditation exercise you would be given the general instruction to watch your breathing, and then be left on your own. But what really is your breathing? This Focus Phrase is highly specific, aiming your attention not toward a general idea of breath awareness, but toward an actual feeling, a pure-sensation experience.

Right now, you can feel this sensation in your nose if you tune into it. Yes? You're pulling the atmosphere of the planet into your lungs through your nose, and then blowing that air out again into the atmosphere. This ongoing act is what keeps you alive, so tuning into your breath experience tunes you directly into your experience of being a living being on this planet; it's a wake-up process.

That's the power of successful affirmations: They aim your attention toward doing something that you can actually accomplish in the present moment.

As you experiment with saying this Focus Phrase to yourself, you'll discover that when you turn your mind's attention toward the experience of your breathing, you aim a spotlight directly onto the emerging present moment—you snap out of thoughts and imaginations of past and future, and re-enter the eternal here and now, where reality actually unfolds.

Because each emerging moment by definition has never happened before, you'll always have a new experience.

Now we're getting closer to the goal of passing through the quiet-mind portal into the Silence. The next essential step is to expand your awareness to include the sensations in your nose as you continue breathing, and also at the same time the inner movement sensations being generated lower in your chest and belly as you inhale and exhale.

As you expand your awareness in this natural process, your mind will naturally let go of busy everyday thoughts and concerns ("point fixation") as you focus on two or more sensations at the same time—which, as we saw, will almost instantly shift you into a more receptive, intuitive, creative mode of consciousness.

Just say to yourself on your next exhale:

"I also feel the movements in my chest and belly."

Go ahead and say this Focus Phrase to yourself and experience how the process of saying these words immediately aims your attention exactly where we want it to go, down and away from past and future thinking, toward quiet, organic, life-affirming present-moment experience.

Again, notice that the careful selection of words in the Focus Phrase continues to focus your attention specifically on physical sensations—in this case the host of movement sensations experienced in your muscles and skin as your torso expands and contracts during each new breathing cycle.

You are being challenged to continue experiencing the airflow sensations in your nose while you also expand your awareness to include a multitude of sensations in your chest and belly as you breathe.

This is a psychological judo move to help you transcend your usual thinking habits. You simply can't stay lost in past and future thoughts while also expanding your awareness to experience more than two distinct sensations at the same time.

You'll probably find that, at first, your attention will try to jump around like crazy from one sensation to the next, until later today, or tomorrow, or next week, you suddenly experience that primal desired shift in awareness from "point fixation" to "experiencing the whole at once."

Welcome to the Silence, wherein your connection with the Source can be experienced. This will benefit you greatly.

Note that when you're lost in thought, you're essentially "not here" in that you're not aware of your own physical presence in the here and now. In just a few breaths, once you get good at this quiet-mind process, you can bring yourself back to the present moment (which is where all manifestation actually happens) and experience your ongoing participation in the unfolding of this new moment. This is so important because, as we'll see later, insight and empowerment from the Universal Mind flows into your personal consciousness only in the present moment.

So if you want to access inspiration, information, guidance, and power, you simply must regularly bring your focus of attention back to the present moment in your own body, so that you're present to receive that inflow.

Please don't be discouraged if, in your first few run-throughs with this Focus Phrase, your focus of attention does jump from one sensation to another, rather than expanding to experience the whole; this is to be expected, so be patient with yourself. The mental habit of chronic "thinking about" (deductive reasoning) rather than experiencing the whole at once (intuitive/integrative insight) is deeply ingrained. Only through repeatedly moving through this quiet-mind process will you begin to develop a new habit.

Once you get good at this shift into intuitive quiet-mind awareness, you'll find you can say these two breath-awareness Focus Phrases to yourself on two consecutive breaths, and almost instantly enter into the Silence.

There's a third Focus Phrase that rounds out this process. Once you've shifted into experiencing the air flowing in and out of your nose plus the movements in your chest and belly as you breathe, you'll find that your attention has expanded to include your head, your belly, your solar plexus, and your heart. Why not go the full distance, into being aware of your whole body at once here in this present moment?

"I'm aware of my whole body, here in this present moment."

Insight and empowerment from the Universal Mind or Creative Spirit flow into your body in the present moment. To maximize your reception of this inflow, it's wise to make sure you're "at home" to receive, and that's what this "whole body" Focus Phrase ensures, that you're fully present and conscious.

Say it. Do it.

To complete this quiet-mind section of the daily manifestation process, there is one more very helpful Focus Phrase that will ensure your success with the process. Again the statement of intent is short and clear and powerful:

"My mind is quiet . . . I am now in the Silence."

Say these words to yourself as you exhale, and as you inhale experience your mind becoming fully quiet. It's that simple, and that profound!

You are now solidly into the learning process of memorizing and mastering the first part of Haanel's manifestation process, that of focusing your attention toward positive feelings and then turning inward to enter the Silence that links you with your higher manifestation powers. As you'll discover in action, the "I choose to enjoy this moment" Focus Phrase will quite naturally encourage you to fully enjoy the breathing sensations that you tune into, so you immediately do feel better!

The next set of Focus Phrases that will consciously focus and activate your manifestation powers will be built solidly upon this joyful quiet-mind foundation.

Note that while moving through a manifestation session, it will be absolutely essential that you never let go of a heightened ongoing awareness of your breathing. Even while you expand your awareness to include specific manifestation dimensions, you must continue to stay aware of the air flowing in and out of your nose and the movements in your chest and belly as you breathe—that's the key to success!

Whenever you lose breath awareness, it's essential to immediately go back to the beginning and re-establish this breath focus.

Note also that Focus Phrases in general are designed to be "said" silently to yourself, not out loud. However, Focus Phrases have no real power if they're simply "thought"—you need to feel the subliminal movements in your tongue, throat, and lips, even though you don't audibly vocalize.

Say to yourself the statement of intent as you exhale . . . then as you inhale, right in the middle of your breath experience, be open to experience the impact of the words throughout your inner awareness. That's how to tap the power of Focus Phrases.

QUIET-MIND PROCESS

Entering the Silence

Here's the quiet mind process as a complete unit for you to memorize and master. In the next chapter we'll explore what to do after you successfully enter into the Silence.

"I choose to focus enjoyably inward."

"I feel the air flowing in and out of my nose."

"I also feel the movements in my chest and belly."

"I'm aware of my whole body, here in this present moment."

"My mind is quiet . . . I am now in the Silence."

Entering the Silence

Practice Suggestions

All too often, we tend to approach manifestation as "no fun" work that we must force ourselves to do in order to achieve our goals. Yes, we must be diligent and persevere toward fulfilling our intent. But the spirit in which we approach manifestation needs to remain light, uplifting, enthusiastic, confident, and enjoyable.

Your challenge in the next days is to remember to remember, and to move through the Focus Phrases many times each day so that you internalize them, develop a new positive mental focusing habit, and master the fine art of waking up your own power to create the life you desire. Haanel is emphatic about the need to practice:

> Persistence will win, but persistence requires that you practice these exercises every day without fail.

What you'll probably discover as you begin practicing these first Focus Phrases is that (a) you have a hard time remembering to pause and move through the process, (b) you sometimes can't remember what the Focus Phrases are, and (c) even after saying the first Focus Phrase to yourself, your thinking mind will yank your attention away from the Focus Phrases and plunge your attention back into past and future mentation.

What to do?

1. **Write them down.** Take a few moments to physically write down the five Focus Phrases on paper or type them into a mobile device if you have one. The act of writing these statements of intent will help you to memorize them—and then you'll also have a copy of the Focus Phrases in hand to aid your memory when needed.

2. **Schedule them.** Decide to move through the quiet-mind process three times each morning, three times each afternoon, and once in the evening—or whatever schedule you prefer. What's important is to commit yourself to the learning process, so that you do this exercise often enough to get to the payoff and new mental habit. Commitment is key to manifestation success, so let's start here!

3. **Play the game.** With your list and schedule in hand, you're now ready to play the Entering the Silence game.

Entering the Silence Game

I'd like to teach you a way to turn the practice and memorization needed to master this process into a continually enjoyable experience. This game will highlight the fact that the very first Focus Phrases, in and of themselves, are remarkably powerful in transforming your moment-to-moment experience.

The goal of this game is to get through the list of five Focus Phrases in one sitting, without looking at your list as you move through the process.

To start, remember to remember to pause and take out your list of Focus Phrases if you need it and read through the list—then put the list away!

First, sit quietly for a few breaths to let the mental dust settle; then without effort, bring the first two words of the first Focus Phrase to mind, and say them to yourself:

"I choose . . ."

Now see if the next three words come to mind effortlessly, and if they do, say them to yourself:

". . . to focus enjoyably . . ."

Now your mind is focusing directly toward your root intent: to experience pleasure and serenity, fulfillment and happiness. And where specifically are you going to focus? Allow the last word to pop into your mind:

"... *inward.*"

Then, after saying these potent elicitor words, just relax a moment and experience the impact of this first Focus Phrase as you breathe, and perhaps say the Focus Phrase again to yourself until it fills your mind with clear intent.

Next, without looking at your list, and without mental effort, see if you remember the theme of the next Focus Phrase: breath awareness. All you need to do is to turn your attention to your nose, and see if the first two words of the second Focus Phrase come to mind. When they do, say these two words to yourself:

"*I feel* ..."

This is a very powerful elicitor statement, which shifts your mind's attention from thinking mode to feeling mode. And now that you're tuned into feeling in your nose, see if the next two words come to mind. What do you feel?

"... *the air* ..."

And what is the air continually doing?

"... *flowing in and out of my nose.*"

Go ahead and take time to experience this breath sensation in your nose, for one or more breaths.

Finally, now that you have the general idea of how to approach each new Focus Phrase, you can continue with the next three on your list in this same manner. But whenever you need to look to your list, the rules of the game say that you must return to the beginning, and start over. Why?

Because the quiet-mind experience needs to start at the beginning each time you move through it, for full impact.

The end of the game is when you do manage to make it to the final quiet-mind Focus Phrase. You can then just sit quietly in the Silence for as long as you choose, remaining aware of your breathing throughout. As Haanel puts it:

Go into the Silence, and know the Truth.

If you play by the rules and don't look at your list while saying the Focus Phrases to yourself, you will find that often, long before you get to the end of this game, your attention has wandered and dropped you back into everyday thoughts or imaginations. This is what makes this game fun: catching yourself drifting and mastering the focusing game of making it all the way to the end, into an immersive experience in Haanel's creative Silence.

Whenever you find that your attention has dropped away from the quiet-mind Focus Phrase experience and slipped into everyday plans, worries, and imaginations, your challenge is to return to the beginning and say to yourself again:

"I choose . . ."

And move through the process again, until you do make it to the end of the fifth Focus Phrase and enter into a unique new experience of inner silence. When you achieve this goal, you've won for the day!

Here's what's so interesting about this whole quiet-mind process: Most of us most of the time don't make it to the end of the game after we start playing it. The challenge seems so simple, and yet our thinking minds are so locked into the "thinking game" that we can't even move through five short sentences and breaths without drifting back into thought. Playing this game will enable you to catch your mind in the act of slipping into relatively unconscious thought.

Often you won't notice that you've dropped out of the game halfway through until minutes or even hours later—and then a flash of awakening will occur. You'll realize that you're not choosing to enjoy the moment, and you'll begin the game at the beginning again, saying that most important Focus Phrase of all:

"I choose to focus enjoyably inward."

After you play this game for a few days, you'll notice that quite remarkable things will happen in your life. You'll find that you are indeed choosing to enjoy each new moment more often, and with greater success.

You are succeeding in changing a core mental habit in the direction of higher awareness and creative pleasure.

You'll find that as you get further and further into winning the game, you strengthen your mental ability to quickly shift into the Silence, and this will allow you to apply the manifestation Focus Phrases of later chapters more effectively.

The beauty of this game is that even when you don't win by getting to the end in one flow, you will win over and over again as you continue to return your attention to the beginning Focus Phrase and choose to enjoy, yet again, the emerging moment.

At some point, the Focus Phrase "I choose to focus enjoyably inward" will become a continual positive background thought in your mind, which in and of itself will bring a deep sense of fulfillment related to your happiness goal.

Here are the Focus Phrases all in one place, so you can copy them longhand onto paper, enter them into your mobile device, or photocopy them to memorize and master:

Entering the Silence

"I choose to focus enjoyably inward."

"I feel the air flowing in and out of my nose."

"I also feel the movements in my chest and belly."

"I'm aware of my whole body, here in this present moment."

"My mind is quiet . . . I am now in the Silence."

Once you practice this expanded version of the process for a while or so, you'll find that you can then shorten the Focus Phrases considerably.

As soon as you say, "I choose to focus enjoyably inward," your attention will naturally focus inward to your breathing experience, and this will naturally lead to a present-moment whole-body awareness, which naturally quiets your habitual thoughts, so that you move right from that Focus Phrase to the quiet-mind Focus Phrase.

That's your goal, and it will take some practice to attain it. Give yourself a couple of weeks before dropping the intermediate Focus Phrases.

❖ 9 ❖

SHIFTING INTO RECEIVE MODE

❦

Haanel strongly encourages us to enter into the Silence. But his guidance on what to do when we attain this inner quiet must be gleaned carefully from his writings, as he gives scant instruction at a practical level as to what to do right when we achieve a quiet mind. For many people who try various techniques based on his teachings, this step in accessing insight and higher guidance often presents a stumbling block that stops further progress.

> Silent thought concentration is the true method of reaching, awakening, and then expressing the wonderful potential power of the world within.

This may be true, but what is "silent thought concentration," and how do we achieve this? In this chapter I'd like to share with you both the psychological understanding and a pragmatic process that I've been exploring for many years, so that you will be able to not only enter into the Silence but achieve "silent thought concentration" each time you pause and move through a manifestation session.

First of all, let's do a quick review of why Haanel considers the quiet-mind phase so important. Here is a compression of his teachings on this point:

> Try to comprehend that Omnipotence itself is absolute silence. It is in the Silence that you get into touch with the omnipotent power of the subconscious mind from which all power is evolved.

Intuition usually comes in the Silence. Great minds seek solitude; it is here that all the larger problems of life are worked out.

Perception will come only in the Silence; this seems to be the condition required for all great purposes.

Inspiration is from within. The Silence offers an ever available and almost unlimited opportunity for awakening the highest conception of Truth.

The Silence is necessary in order to receive the information, inspiration, and wisdom necessary for the development of your purpose.

From this list, we can see that what we want to have happen when we enter the Silence is "to receive." If we are receptive, something will "come" to us—insight awakening, information, wisdom, inspiration, power, intuition, perception, greatness, solutions to problems, and communion with the Divine. What an amazing list of what we can receive—but only if we're open to receive!

For quite some time now, I've been exploring the very nature of "openness to receive," and have coined the term "receive mode" to indicate that there are three modes of consciousness that we can be in: broadcast mode, receive mode, and turned-off mode. I want to talk with you about these three modes of consciousness, because your entire success with this manifestation process depends on being able to shift into receive mode when you enter into the Silence.

As a beginning hint, note that Haanel makes the following statement:

We have seen that every thought is received by the brain, which is the organ of the conscious mind.

He many times says that when we tune into the Universal Mind, we can "receive" inspired thoughts from this greater wisdom and intelligence. This is how we have a flash of creative insight that comes to us fully conceived beyond the bounds of logical deduction; this is how we experience "knowing" and spiritual realization.

There are indeed two sources of thought in the human mind: the biological ego's associative deductive rational thought process, and the intuitive reception of inspired ideas that emerge from an integration of the personal mind's creative function and nonpersonal spiritual inputs.

When in silence you come into possession of a sense of poise and power, you will be ready to receive the information, inspiration, or wisdom which may be necessary for the development of your purpose.

Haanel's "sense of poise" has fascinated me because "poise" is defined as "a state of equilibrium, a dignified, self-confident manner; self-possession and stability." To be poised means to hold a position where we're ready to act at any moment, but are presently calm and balanced and awaiting—alert but relaxed.

To be in tune with eternal truth we must possess poise and harmony within. In order to receive intelligence the receiver must be in tune with the transmitter.

Here we have another hint about the quality of mind we want to nurture when we enter the Silence: We must have "poise and harmony within." When we quiet all our usual disruptive thoughts and focus on enjoying the present moment, we shift into a harmonious mood, as we learned in the previous chapters. But here we have a new thought: "In order to receive intelligence the receiver must be in tune with the transmitter."

Clearly, we must shift from being in broadcast mode, where we're the transmitter, into receive mode, where we're alert and receptive and focused directly toward the source of our inspiration and information.

How can you accomplish this goal, this shift into receive mode, each time you do a manifestation session? The answer is found once again in stating your intent as a very carefully worded Focus Phrase, so that your conscious mind turns its focus of attention exactly where needed: tuned in with the transmitter.

The best Focus Phrase we've developed to instantly provoke this shift into receive mode with attention fully aimed at the Source is this:

"I am open to receive guidance from my Source."

This is a perfect statement of intent. It's short, it generates a feeling of openness, and it aims your attention toward the inner wellspring of human inspiration and empowerment. You simply say the words to yourself and hold them in your mind and heart, and they will effortlessly resonate deep within your being and generate a unique inner experience.

Remember that Focus Phrases will have no power at all unless you continually remain aware of your breathing experience at the same time that you say the Focus Phrase to yourself.

You must "be here" as a physical presence if you're going to receive, and breath awareness is the indicator that you're here in the present moment, ready to receive.

Also, as we've seen, your mental chatter must stop in order for you to receive higher-order insights. When you're thinking habitual everyday ego-driven thoughts originating in your own brain, you are locked in broadcast mode—and you cannot be in broadcast mode and receive mode at the same time; that's one of the core laws of communication. Unfortunately most of us most of the time are busy thinking and therefore in broadcast mode, which means that most of the time, we simply aren't in receive mode—and therefore insights cannot reach us.

That's why regularly pausing for at least a few moments to move through the quiet-mind process can transform your life, because you're regularly shifting into receive mode, where the real gold is found in consciousness.

The world within is the Universal Fountain of supply, and the world without is the outlet to the stream. Our ability to receive depends upon our recognition of this Universal Fountain, this Infinite Energy of which each individual is an outlet.

Haanel sees individual people as outlets for the divine flow of love and harmony, information and insight. All of life is a flow, and what is required of us is "our recognition of this Universal Fountain, this Infinite Energy." And to recognize something, we must turn our attention toward it and experience its reality. "Be still, and know that I am God."

First comes the act of silencing our mental chatter and shifting into receive mode. Then comes the remarkable human act of realizing what we're seeing before us. From this realization comes the knowing, and from the knowing comes the inflow of exactly what we need in our lives to live the good life attuned to God. As we quoted in the beginning, a single idea may be worth millions of dollars, and these ideas can come only to those who are receptive, who are prepared to receive them, and who are in a successful frame of mind.

Again we come to this notion of the frame of mind, the prevailing mood and attitude that you bring into the Silence. We've seen that "successful" for Haanel means being in a "happy and harmonious" state of mind. As you practice the quiet-mind part of this manifestation process, you'll find that the breath and whole-body awareness Focus Phrases will naturally help shift you into this positive frame of mind.

Then you say to yourself the specific receive mode Focus Phrase: "I am open to receive guidance from my Source." Stay aware of your breathing and whole-body presence, and relax into the Silence as you wait in a state of poise for the inflow of whatever information and empowerment might be available to you at that time. Here's another way Haanel explains this:

> The next step is to place yourself in position to receive this insight or power. As it is omnipresent, it must be within you. All power is from within.

Again we return to the notion that the insight, information, power, or guidance you seek is not coming from somewhere off in heaven or outside of you. Insight is a function of consciousness, which as we've seen operates outside the space-time continuum. You must aim your attention directly inward to your own center if you want to find the Universal Center. Your personal center and the Universal Center are one and the same—that's the whole point! This means that you are never separated from your Source, except to the extent that you fail to aim your attention inward and open up to receive.

> You must be receptive, and this receptivity is acquired just as physical strength is gained, by exercise.

Often we assume that being receptive is an innate quality, but here Haanel states clearly just the opposite—that "receptivity is acquired." I have found this to be entirely true. This means that the first time you do a manifestation session, you can't expect the angels to sing instantly to you in four-part harmony. You must exercise and develop your ability to receive, just as you would exercise to develop a capacity in sports.

Opening to receive is not just a lofty idea; it's a pragmatic process that you nurture and master. So your challenge ahead is to take time to move through a manifestation session quite often, perhaps three or four times a day, so that you develop your "receptivity muscle" and become strong in the art of receiving.

From this process of self-contemplation comes inspiration, which is creative intelligence.

When you look inward toward your inner Source, you are indeed contemplating your own higher existence. And this inward-looking will prove a process of continual discovery, because you and the Universal Mind are one, which means that you yourself are infinite. That's a giant notion. I challenge you to explore this concept through personal experience to discover if it is true for you.

As you open to receive while in the Silence, it's important to let go of expectations of your ego and to shift into more of a sensory or feeling mode of consciousness. Don't expect anything—just let yourself focus on feeling attuned to your infinite inner center of consciousness as you "touch the Universal Mind" with your own presence. Focus your attention not on the idea of your Creative Source, but on the actual feeling of being connected with this infinite presence that we call God or Divine Presence.

By whatever name, what's key is that you turn your attention directly inward to your own center, which is the connection point with the divine, and actually tune into experience the feeling of your connection.

You'll benefit here greatly by using the neutral word "Source" rather than "God" or any other religious term related to the ineffable Infinite Divine Creative Presence, because this neutral term sets you free to discover, through direct inner experience, what this Source truly is as an intimate inner feeling, not a traditional theological concept.

For Haanel, "feeling connected" is definitely key to success and deeper happiness, because our human feelings are the experiential passageway that energetically connects us with the Universal Mind. As we've seen, he identifies the subjective emotional realm of consciousness as our link with the Divine. Through this "feeling" link, transmissions from the Universal Mind flow in and are then processed by our personal minds and experienced as inspired thoughts, solutions, or realizations.

In this perspective, your challenge is to learn how to shift out of thinking mode into feeling mode more and more often. This is the manifestation-portal event.

As you shift from thinking to feeling, you pass through a portal into a new dimension. Here's a perhaps startling psychological fact: Linear deductive reasoning is actually a collapsed reality of only two dimensions. If you reflect a moment, you'll realize that there's no volume to analytical thought, no sense of depth at all. As cognitive scientists point out, our everyday thinking is a point-to-point linear mental process—it's a line through time.

Only when you temporarily quiet that habitual linear type of thinking do you pop once again into the volume of your senses and the experiential present moment, and regain the experience of real participation with the real world, which is where all manifestation occurs.

As you get good at quieting your mind and focusing inward in a receptive mood, you'll find that you often pop spontaneously into a truly expanded quality of consciousness, where there exists an infinity of dimensions. And this isn't just a way of talking; this can be a direct and utterly marvelous inner experience.

> Spirit is omnipresent, ever ready; all that is required is a proper recognition of its omnipotence and a willingness or desire to become the recipient of its beneficent effects. Then you will find that the things you seek are seeking you.

I mentioned earlier the new vision and research of scientists such as Stephen Hawking who state that for the universe to function at all, there must be at least nine coexisting dimensions. They also postulate that every square inch of space throughout the universe is filled with matter and anti-matter, and that the universe itself is a vast, intelligent, harmonious being in which everything is connected, beyond the space-time continuum, with everything else.

Haanel a hundred years ago seems to have had a direct vision of this expanded reality. He realized somehow that everything in the universe is connected with the Creative Source that brought this entire reality into being, and it's this direct, intimate, organic sense of connection that he encourages you to open up and plug into so that you "become the recipient of its beneficent effects" where "the things you seek are seeking you."

Let's end this chapter focusing on the pragmatics of all this.

STEP 3: OPEN TO RECEIVE

Let's move through what you've learned thus far: the three main Focus Phrases that take you beyond ideas directly into experiencing the receive mode state of consciousness. In the next chapter we'll explore what to do after you successfully enter into the Silence. (Please remember to move through the three breath/whole-body steps that quiet your thoughts to lead you into "I am now in the Silence," until this quiet-mind process becomes natural to you.)

1. *"I choose to focus enjoyably inward."*

2. *"My mind is quiet . . . I am now in the Silence."*

3. *"I am open to receive guidance from my Source."*

❖ 10 ❖

CLARIFY YOUR CORE DESIRES

❧❦❧

Most people assume that personal willpower and mental focusing generate the action leading toward manifestation. But as we've seen, Charles Haanel's writings, when read carefully, insist that thought alone can accomplish nothing new or creative. He says over and over that the driving power of manifestation is passion, emotion, desire—in sum, strong positive feeling.

In this chapter I want to teach you how to advance, while still in the Silence, into a sharp focus on experiencing your most important passion and desire at any moment. As you might guess, now that you've read this far into this book, at some point I'll introduce you to a special Focus Phrase that will generate the focus we aim for here.

In each manifestation session that you pause and move through, hopefully at least once a day, you will reach the point with this fourth Focus Phrase where you are able to look inward, observe your core passion at the moment, and decide through this process which driving intent to focus your power of attention upon during the session.

Often you'll find that the same passion and related goal returns over and over, for days or even weeks or months, until that goal and yearning is attained and fulfilled, but probably you'll find that you have more than one goal that you're advancing toward, step by step.

In traditional Buddhist, Hindu, and even Christian theologies, the very notion of desire carries a negative connotation. Most meditative and contemplative practices insist that desires of any kind are bad for the soul and must be repressed and put forcefully away if one is to attain spiritual awakening and fulfillment.

Haanel's system flies in the face of these beliefs, and it does so in a very specific way. He insists, as we began to explore earlier, that manifestation is driven by our feelings, our desires, and our yearnings, and that we will manifest nothing without bringing them to the fore. Again, here's the key quote:

A thought's vitality depends upon the feeling with which the thought is impregnated. If the thought is passionate and constructive, it will possess vitality; it will have life; it will grow, develop, expand; it will be creative; it will attract to itself everything necessary for its complete development.

Notice the word that he uses: "impregnated." That's a powerful way to state his meaning, because impregnation comes from the sexual act of creation, and it's the feeling that is the impregnator and the thought that is the receptive host. Wow.

And what are the "feeling" qualities that he specifically names for successful impregnation of a thought? Passionate and constructive.

"Passionate." What does that word convey to us? The dictionary defines passionate as "easily aroused; having, compelled by, ruled by, or expressing intense or vehement emotion or strong feeling."

Haanel asks you to focus inward, quiet your mind, look directly to your Source, open to receive higher guidance, and then tune into your most passionate yearning or desire at the moment.

Notice that the order here is crucial and psychologically astute. If you just suddenly try to identify your dominant passion, you're going to be looking with your everyday awareness, and who knows what you'll find.

Haanel requests that you first move through a serious meditative process, tune into your inner guide, and then (and only then) look to see what core passion you want to tap into and use to empower your manifestation process.

So many people, in their quest for successful manifestation of their dreams, fall flat right at this point. They might be driven by a host of conflicting desires fueled by the media, by past programming by their parents or peer group, by distorted ideas of what brings happiness in life. Very often, secondary or temporary hungers dominate their awareness, so that they almost never get a clear look at their deeper hungers, their higher passions, their true desires and needs.

For quite a number of years I've been looking closely at the whole phenomenon that we call "hunger" and "need" and "desire." Surely we all hunger for food to keep our physical bodies alive and well. We hunger for sexual intimacy and release. We crave stimulation when understimulated for too long, and yearn for peace and quiet when overstimulated for too long. We need a roof over our heads, a community to support us when we are in trouble, and regular bouts of frivolous play and entertainment.

Most animals share with us most of these needs. They're in fact programmed into our brains and drive us toward satisfactions of many different kinds. Usually we fixate on attaining secondary material expressions of our true desires—but often we remain unsatisfied deep down.

Haanel says it this way:

If we think of some form of material wealth, we may secure it. By concentrated thought the required conditions will be brought about and the proper effort put forth, which will result in bringing about the circumstances necessary to realize our desires. But we often find that when we secure the things we thought we wanted, they do not have the effect we expected. That is, the satisfaction is only temporary, or possibly is the reverse of what we expected.

That's surely the universal experience of our advertisement-driven culture, in which we're actually led to believe that Coke's the thing, that a fancy car will solve all our problems, and that white teeth will answer all our romantic needs. Much of the shallow dimensions of the New Age movement were driven by what was called "spiritual materialism," in which people were led to believe that by grabbing onto high beliefs and esoteric practices, a deeper spiritual hunger could be satisfied.

In this chapter I want to challenge you to look more deeply toward the desires and passions you carry within you, so that you can clearly identify the underlying passion that drives you and focus specifically on satisfying that deeper itch, not the surface tingle.

There are without question a list of basic needs that all human beings share, and that we all need to focus on and satisfy, in order to be happy and harmonious in our lives. Here's the outline that Haanel offers:

We cannot be happy unless we have health, strength, congenial friends, pleasant environment, and sufficient supply not only to take care of our necessities, but also to provide for those comforts and luxuries to which we are entitled.

Do you agree with his list? If so, when you look within to see what needs you have that require attention and manifestation, be sure to reflect on the following:

1. Are you physically healthy, or do you need to focus on healing and dietary and lifestyle changes?

2. Are you emotionally healthy, or does this need focused attention?

3. Are you strong, or feeling weak? Does this dimension of your life need attention?

4. Do you have deep friendships that nurture you? Do you feel adequately loved and appreciated? Or do you need to focus on bringing this congenial friends element to the fore?

5. Is your living and work environment harmonious and healthy, or are you stuck in an environment that grates on your nerves and erodes your sense of aesthetics and health?

6. Materially, do you have enough money and sources to obtain what you need so that you have good shelter, good food, and all the rest of the material possessions that you need?

7. Also, because we're here not only to survive but to thrive and enjoy life, are you making enough money, living in the proper community, and working at the proper job, so you can access the beyond-subsistence things you are entitled to?

This list can be shortened in your daily meditation to:

1. Health

2. Emotions

3. Power

4. Friendships

5. Environment

6. Survival

7. Pleasure

If you look deep within you and find one of these shouting for attention, definitely give it attention. Basic needs require regular attention to make sure you're keeping everything in balance. If you deny or ignore anything on this list, you're liable to get into compulsive behavior and avoidance patterns, such as drugs. Best to listen and respond with action.

But notice that Haanel lists these needs with the preface that we need to satisfy these needs in order to satisfy a deeper desire, in order to be happy. The driving intent is not to have a fancy house or flashy job; the intent is to fulfill temporary material needs in order to fulfill your deeper hunger, to experience enduring inner harmony and contentment. And usually, only when all of these needs are taken care of can you feel harmonious in your mind, your heart, and your relationships.

So do focus and manifest anything on that list of seven, so that you regularly experience the underlying emotion of happiness that comes with satisfying your human needs. But throughout, remember that you will need to focus on and sustain positive thoughts in order to manifest what you need in life. As Haanel says:

> A happy thought cannot exist in an unhappy consciousness; therefore the consciousness must change.

So before you attempt to manifest something external that you hope will make you feel better inside, you're going to have to deal with any negative inner thoughts and feelings that are predictably manifesting the outer negatives in your life.

What Inner Feeling Do You Hunger For?

As mentioned before, Haanel encourages us to not focus our manifestation energy on specific outward things that might be part of our desired happiness picture. Instead he suggests strongly that we look deep within, find the core positive yearning that's living under pressure in our hearts, and focus on manifesting that positive feeling, not as a future imagination, but as a present-moment experience inside us.

Please bear with me—this requires close attention to see adequately into the spiritual logic of this process. Yearning is a power under pressure. There is something that you hunger for, that you need, but that externally you don't have. However, that exact feeling inside you of yearning for something indicates that you already know this feeling, and want more of it in your life, yes?

Haanel insists, and I with him, that what we ultimately want is the feeling of being one with our Creator, of not feeling separated from God's love. Everything else is a secondary yearning, wouldn't you agree?

And here's the joke: If we can yearn for a feeling, that means we already have a vague connection with that feeling. We're already plugged into happiness and harmony. But we've let the connection be mostly lost, in all our various negative attitudes and beliefs and judgments and all the rest. Our problem in feeling bad isn't external. The problem is that our internal condition is generating a negative outside world.

So we're back where we started a few pages ago—as Haanel put it earlier, "the consciousness must change" for the better if we want our external situation to change for the better. And how do we change our consciousness?

Once again, our ego minds cannot think us out of our ingrained attitudes and negative beliefs and emotions. Remember the adage, often attributed to Albert Einstein: "You can't solve a problem with the same kind of thinking that created the problem in the first place." Something new is needed, an inflow of fresh ideas, of more positive thoughts. And where do these come from?

From your Source. It's plain and simple, but so many intelligent people fail to get this very simple point. Inspiration is our godsend, as they say. Insight from our deeper source of wisdom is required to break us out of our mental habits and to impregnate our usual thoughts with higher realization and a better game plan.

And notice that that's exactly what we're doing here, and that's why I have suggested you first look inward, quiet your usual thoughts, enter the

Silence, and open up to receive guidance from your Source before you look to your yearnings and see what the core yearning really is that you need to work to satisfy.

I suspect that there is a passionate pressure inside you right now—otherwise you wouldn't be motivated to read this book right now. If you can look directly inward and make contact with that passion, you will tap the power and energy that will then impregnate your thoughts with insight, wisdom, practical plans, and step-by-step procedures to begin to manifest not just a car or a house or a job, but an entire life that is an expression of your inner yearning.

The yearning ultimately comes from your Creator or Source, by whatever name. The yearning is to not only subsist and survive for a while on this planet; the yearning is to fulfill your purpose on this planet. People who have identified their purpose, tapped their deepest yearning, and welcomed Spirit into their hearts and minds to manifest their purpose are happy people.

Do you want to be one of these people?

If so, here's what you do.

As a regular daily habit, even hourly if you want to, you must remember to remember to pause, shift your attention to present-moment sensory experiences so that you temporarily quiet your regular thoughts, and enter into the Silence.

And as you breathe into that quiet-mind state of consciousness where Universal Mind can merge with your individual mind, say to yourself, "I am open to receive guidance from my Source."

And as you stay aware of your breathing, just see what comes to you, as an experience, right in the middle of your breathing experience—that's where Spirit flows in!

At some point, when you're ready, you can use a special Focus Phrase that will gently awaken a realization inside you, of what you really desire deep down to bring into your life. Let the words of the Focus Phrase, in and of themselves, elicit a response and realization within you.

Simply say to yourself the following Focus Phrase:
"I know what I want."

Say the words, and at the same time continue to stay aware of your breathing experience in your nose, your chest, and your belly.

Most people most of the time do not know what they really need to be truly happy. You can begin to evolve into a person who does know what you want.

THE REAL SECRET

Most people, when they ask themselves what they want, think of a thing they want to possess and do something with. If you look inside and say, "I know what I want," and what you want is an ice cream bar, fine, don't belittle small desires—go get one!

But if you're this deep into this particular book, what you're looking for probably isn't a box of chocolate or any other temporary fix to push back your sense of frustration or incompleteness. You know you need something deeper than just another thing, or more of the things you already have. If you're in need of something, fine—this program will help you focus and manifest that thing. But there's a deeper dimension to satisfying your needs.

My experience in this regard (which runs parallel with Haanel's) is that what we really need to bring into our lives isn't a thing; it's a feeling, an inner experience.

If you say to yourself, "I need more . . ." and complete the sentence, what words come to mind?

Sometimes, you'll find your inner voice saying, "I need more money," and this will very possibly be a valid need—and this program will help you manifest that financial need.

Sometimes your voice might say, "I need more love," and this is definitely a serious yearning to respond to.

Perhaps you ask yourself what you truly desire, and your inner response (guided by the Universal Mind, which does know what you need) will say, "I need better health" or "I need to feel safe and free from all my worries."

But deeper down, always, what I'm hungering for is a shift in my feelings—I yearn to feel more of a core good feeling. That's the secret: What we truly yearn for, beyond things and situations, is the deeper positive feeling that these things and situations might bring us.

If you at first say to yourself that you need a better-paying job or a more fulfilling relationship, this is fine, but then look deeper. Look to see how you feel now in your heart, related to that need. And then look to see what feeling you hunger to feel inside you that a new job or relationship or whatever would hopefully bring you. Perceive the core yearning!

BASIC MANIFESTATION LOGIC

Let's take a closer look at Haanel's statement that began this chapter's discussion:

> A thought's vitality depends upon the feeling with which the thought is impregnated. If the thought is passionate and constructive, it will possess vitality; it will have life; it will grow, develop, expand; it will be creative; it will attract to itself everything necessary for its complete development.

You have the thought, "What I need is to lose ten pounds." Good, that's a thought that seems to represent a solid need or intent. But the thought on its own will accomplish nothing, because "a thought's vitality depends upon the feeling with which the thought is impregnated."

And where is that essential passionate and constructive feeling going to be found and tapped? That's the logic that you must return to over and over in this program. How do you access the feeling that will impregnate your thought and intent, so that your intent will grow, develop, expand, be creative, and attract everything necessary for its complete development?

You are, essentially, beyond all your thoughts and beliefs and ideas and judgments, a feeling deep inside your chest. But to gain power, you must learn to focus regularly and steadily and positively on that core feeling, that dynamic yearning, and impregnate your manifestation thoughts with the passionate power of that feeling!

AGAIN, THE PROCESS

Here's what I often experience when I move through the manifestation process: I choose to look enjoyably inward, and I focus on my breathing to quiet my mind. This inner action of focusing in my chest area naturally brings me into deep encounter with the current feelings in my heart. I breathe into these feelings that are found right at the center of my heart experience, and then say to myself, "I am open to receive guidance from my Source," and tune into whatever new experience comes to me, from that deeper Source. And as I focus on that experience, I say to myself, "I know what I want."

Perhaps as I'm saying those words, I don't yet really know what I'm yearning for that day, but in the process of stating that "I know what I want," insight comes flowing into my mind from a deep source, and suddenly I do know!

That's what insight is all about. That's the "aha!" experience that is required right at this point. Perhaps in the first week or so of learning this process you won't have a flash of insight into your deeper needs. But trust me, at some point soon, you will. You'll make that vital inner "feeling" connection that carries the power to impregnate and activate your thoughts.

Again, I welcome you to move through the process yourself. As Haanel regularly said, it's essential to exercise the mental muscle in order to become strong in this process. Each time you pause and say these Focus Phrases to yourself, you're moving deeper into the Manifestation Process that will bring you what you desire.

Be sure to make your breath experience primary, and after you say each Focus Phrase, take time (one or more breaths) to open up and experience the resonance of the intent statement as it awakens deep feelings and insights within you, bringing your unconscious Universal Mind into full play.

1. *"I choose to focus enjoyably inward."*

2. *"My mind is quiet . . . I am now in the Silence."*

3. *"I am open to receive guidance from my Source."*

4. *"I know what I want."*

❖ 11 ❖

Tap the Creative Source

❖❖❖

In many ways this chapter is the heart of this book. I want to talk deeper than I ever have before in print about what it means to feel connected with your Creative Source. And I want to complete the progression you've step by step been learning, to where you are indeed face to face with Universal Mind. I'll do my best to keep my psychologist's hat on for the duration of this ride, but it's going to push the limits of scientific discourse and then some for us to actually delve into the process of looking directly into the face of our Creator. Don't blink!

Consider this quote from Haanel:

By plainly stating to the subconscious mind certain specific things to be accomplished, forces are set in operation that lead to the result desired. Here is a source of power which places us in touch with Omnipotence. This is a deep principle well worth our most earnest study.

This is of course what Focus Phrases do: They plainly state to the unconscious mind specific things to be accomplished. I hope you're beginning to perceive that there's a multistep process taking place each time you state a Focus Phrase to yourself. First comes the remembrance of the Focus Phrase as a statement of intent. Then comes the actual inner vocalization of the statement of intent. At this point, your unconscious mind receives the request of the conscious mind, and it responds immediately.

Then comes the rising up of that response into consciousness, as a flash of insight, a realization, a special feeling, or a coherent thought.

When you say to yourself, "I feel the air flowing in and out of my nose," chances are you are *not* right at that moment in fact tuned into that sensory event. But as soon as you speak the intent to focus there, the unconscious mind responds and focuses your attention there. And after you speak your intent in the Focus Phrase, you immediately experience this shift in focus and become aware of the air flowing in and out of your nose.

Each Focus Phrase moves you through this process. On your exhale you say the statement of intent to yourself, and on your next inhale you experience the response of your deeper self to this statement of intent. The conscious ego speaks the words, the unconscious mind responds, and the conscious ego then experiences that response.

WHOM ARE YOU TALKING TO?

Let's be clear: In the act of speaking "to yourself" you are indeed speaking to your unconscious mind, to that vast realm of your being that exists just below or beyond your conscious awareness. The purpose of Focus Phrases in general is to stimulate this act of communication between the conscious and unconscious realms of the mind.

As already mentioned, Haanel firmly believes that your unconscious mind is your direct link with the Divine. And by speaking an intent to the unconscious mind, you are therein communicating your desire and intent to God.

That's pretty heavy stuff.

And that's exactly where true power to manifest comes from: your ability and intent to tap via your unconscious mind into Universal Mind's infinite power and intelligence, which then communicates back via the unconscious to your conscious ego mind, so that you can creatively imagine, visualize, and go into action to achieve a goal in your life.

Haanel saw human beings as infinite creatures with a conscious mind that has the power to aim its attention toward "the world within" in order to tap into an infinite intelligence and power, and then receive guidance from that infinite intelligence and power—and go into action to perform in the outside world and achieve the stated intent.

The world within is the Universal Fountain of supply, and the world without is the outlet to the stream. Our ability to receive depends upon our recognition of this Universal Fountain, this Infinite Energy of which each individual is an outlet.

Here we come to the ultimate challenge, that of tuning into the Universal Fountain, so that we can become an outlet to that source of supply. In order to manifest our desires, we need creative power, agreed? And where are we going to find that creative power? Let's review an important quote from Haanel in which he hits the nail on the head:

Creative power does not originate in the individual, but in the Universal, which is the source and foundation of all energy and substance; the individual is simply the channel for the distribution of this energy.

I want to keep returning to this basic notion until I'm sure it's fully understood and accepted in your own mind and heart: It's a myth to think that you as a separate ego body can accomplish anything new or creative at all. Yes, you can plug into the existing machine and habitually perform actions that generate results. But if you want to change your life for the better, you're going to have to do something creative, to bring into being a reality that did not exist before.

If you believe that you exist as an isolated bubble of awareness with no connection or dependence upon anything beyond or higher than yourself, of course this book will have no meaning, and you won't have read even this far into it without tossing it aside. So I assume you do experience in your life a greater reality than your ego bubble usually acknowledges. What we're doing here is learning how to regularly shift focus so as to look directly to your greater self; call it the Universal Mind or God or whatever other name you like.

I'm not a great fan of building abstract belief castles in the sky. I prefer to cut to the chase, and that's what we do with the next Focus Phrase in this manifestation process. If you want to access higher wisdom and empowerment and all the rest, what do you need? State that need clearly, as if it's already a done deal, and your unconscious mind will respond by doing what you request. Come on, let's admit it—we want to experience that core feeling of being connected with our Creative Source. Who wants to feel disconnected from their Source? Who wants to feel out of touch with their Creator?

You are seeking the power to change your life for the better. Say it. Do it.

"I feel connected with creative power."

Say these words to yourself, and let them reverberate throughout your being, aiming your mind's attention directly inward to establish a connection that you feel!

And what do you do now?

Please note carefully: You do nothing at all. You are in receive mode. You are open to receive whatever comes to you in this deep meditative state. That's what meditation is, after all: the entering into a quiet-mind quality of consciousness where you are tuned into your breathing first and foremost, because it will be right in the middle of your breathing that you will receive the inflow coming from the Universal into your individual mind.

Perhaps you stay in this meditative receptive mode of consciousness for one breath, for one minute, for one hour. It doesn't matter. Stay there a while, enjoy the bliss of being plugged into the Divine, and with your breathing as your medium of receptivity, allow new feelings, perhaps new thoughts, new whatever, to come flooding or seeping or flowing into your conscious mind.

"I feel connected with creative power."

RECEIVING THE VISION

Let's review again what we've explored thus far in this manifestation process, so that you can see the logic leading to the next step: (1) You've learned to use Focus Phrases to redirect your attention so as to quiet your mind and (2) open up to guidance from your higher Source; (3) through the influence of this guidance, you've tuned into the deeper yearnings and feelings in your heart so that you know what you really need right now; and (4) you've connected at the core feeling level with your creative source of power and inspiration.

Now what happens?

One way or another, now or sometime later, you will receive a flash of insight, a new idea, a vision of where you want to aim your attention so that you bring into being a new quality to your life.

In other words, your conscious mind has requested—even demanded—and then received a power-packed vision from the Universal Mind. You're inspired! Hold in mind what Haanel says about this:

The unlimited creative power of the Universal Mind is within control of the conscious mind of the individual. We can have the inspiration of the omnipotent Universal Mind on demand at any time.

I hope that now you're beginning to see the fully interactive two-way dynamic of this manifestation process. You as an individual have the conscious power to ask for guidance, for insight, for the infinite wisdom of Universal Mind. And Universal Mind by its very nature responds and gives you the information, the power, the vision, and the will to carry out the actions step by step that will manifest the game plan.

Jesus said this so clearly: "Seek and it will be shown to you; ask and it will be given."

But most of us, in opening to receive a vision, expect to receive a vision of our outer physical world being transformed. We want to receive a game plan for manipulating the outer world in order to get what we want. Sometimes this might happen, and at certain stages of manifestation, particular outer-world details might come to us in this receive mode state.

But Haanel strongly advises not to anticipate this type of vision, because it's not going to be big enough to permeate and transform your world with a new experience. Instead, as we've seen already, he insists that we need to use our own conscious minds to manage our attention so that our inner world begins to change for the better. And when the inner changes, the outer naturally changes too. Here's how he puts it:

> The world without is a reflection of the world within. What appears without is what has been found within. Harmony in the world within will be reflected in the world without by harmonious conditions, agreeable surroundings, the best of everything. This inner harmony is the foundation of health and a necessary essential to all greatness, all power, all attainment, all achievement, and all success.

We are really cutting to the chase here, because we're considering the very nature of the vision we seek in order to be truly fulfilled in our lives. If our external world is "a reflection of the world within," then obviously we need to first change our world within if we want to change our outside world.

> The great fact is that the source of all life and all power is found within. This means that the insight, strength, and power to answer our needs will be found within.

Psychologists often point out rather despairingly that it's difficult to change a person's attitudes and inner mental habits, which in turn determine one's inner feelings and condition. Depressed people stay depressed, anxious people stay anxious, prejudiced people stay prejudiced, unhappy and disharmonious people stay that way. Such is life.

Not true, says Haanel. Not true, says John Selby. Not true, say many millions of people who have used their own conscious thoughts in order to positively change their inner lives and thus change their outer lives as well.

Right here is where I love Haanel the most, where he insists that we can rapidly improve our inner condition of harmony and clarity, power and compassion. All we need to do is to regularly move through the process of asking for and manifesting more harmony and love in our inner lives!

INNER HARMONY

When I work with a client in my therapy practice, one of the first things I like to do is to guide this person to the point of realizing what they really want: They want to feel better. That's the core driving desire and yearning that has brought them to see a therapist. They want more inner harmony and peace, they want more insight and love, and they want more trust and strength.

In sum, they want to feel more connected with the true infinite source of all those human feelings—and please note that they are feelings, not abstract ideals or material possessions.

People can do analytical therapy twice a week for twenty years and never really feel any better. They might understand why they have been conditioned to feel like they do, but the thinking mind cannot think itself into better feelings. It must do something ultimately humbling: It must ask for help.

That's what you're doing in this manifestation process: You're asking for help. Your ego mind and your personal conditioned mental and emotional reactions need something beyond themselves in order to let go of all the negativity and fear, the judgment and disharmony, and take the great leap into positive harmonious states of consciousness.

True, the old attitudes and programmings will always be there. Your saving grace is that you don't have to focus your attention in negative directions if you don't want to. In order to receive creative power and manifest your dream, you might need to change your core focusing habit—and without higher help, this can seem impossible to accomplish.

What you need is to tap into a higher vision so that you can actively hold your focus of attention in directions that keep you plugged into the Universal Mind's wisdom, compassion, and harmony. Hold in mind that you are seeking to gain creative power to manifest your deeper needs, and access to this creative power comes only when you choose to manifest a brighter and more positive experience inside your own heart.

We can come into harmonious relationship with the Universal, and when we have accomplished this we may ask anything to which we are entitled, and the way will be clear.

Here we see again Haanel's nonstop insistence on the need to accomplish the inner work and transformation before you can accomplish the outer manifestations. Once inner harmony with the Universal has been accomplished, the outer material fulfillment is relatively easy.

I've seen this happen often in my professional life. A person suffering from inner disharmony, confusion, anxiety, and depression will almost always manifest that kind of negative outer life as well. Social workers struggle so hard, for instance, to help people change their outer lives, but usually fail unless an inner transformation comes first.

But almost like a miracle, some seemingly charmed people are suddenly able to transform their outer lives in harmonious ways. Why? Because they have found inner harmony; they have opened up to their

Creator (not through submission, but through clear positive intent) and asked for the guidance and vision needed to become aligned with the Universal Harmony that is now flooding into their lives because they asked for it.

I assume that you desire fairly rapid positive change in your life. I intend to give you the tools to accomplish this. Once again, take time to reflect on the Focus Phrase you've learned in this chapter, upon the statement of intent that will step by step over the next weeks bring you into full realization of what you really desire to manifest in your life.

1. *"I choose to focus enjoyably inward."*

2. *"My mind is quiet . . . I am now in the Silence."*

3. *"I am open to receive guidance from my Source."*

4. *"I know what I want."*

5. *"I feel connected with creative power."*

❖ 12 ❖

MANIFEST YOUR HIGHER PURPOSE

In the last chapters, you've focused your attention further and further inward, to the point where you find yourself focusing directly upon the Creative Source—the infinite, intelligent, compassionate power that manifested this entire world and universe. That's quite an amazing thing to do, to humbly and courageously see your Creator eye to eye.

I hope you understand that this inward turning to enter the Divine Presence isn't something you just do once and are done with it. This process is a lifelong path to follow, in which every day you return to this inner focus on the Universal and tune into whatever insights and guidance and power you are naturally ready to receive to further your life. And each time you look within, you will open yourself to receive a new experience, because time marches on, and it's always a new moment.

At the end of this book, we'll offer a number of ways in which you can in the next weeks train your mind to move through the first part of the Manifestation Process. We are now ready in our discussion to move on to the final step, in which you once again turn your mind's attention outward and allow Spirit to guide your thinking mind toward manifesting a new vision that you go into action to achieve.

In essence, what you've done in the first part of the process is to shift from your everyday pragmatic conscious mode of consciousness into the equal and opposite function of the mind, the unconscious intuitive spiritual mode of awareness. Now it's time to bring your deeper insights back into conscious focus, so that your thinking mind can merge with your deeper being and generate action to manifest your desire. Remember earlier, when I quoted Haanel as saying:

> It is the coordination of these two centers of our being (conscious and unconscious) which is the great secret of life. With this knowledge we can bring the objective and subjective minds into conscious cooperation and thus coordinate the finite and the infinite.

That's your challenge now: how to do this, how to bring the infinite inspiration and creativity of the Universal Mind down into your individual thoughts and vision. Notice that Haanel talks about "conscious cooperation" between the finite and the infinite. There is to be no ego struggle for dominance here, nor any overpowering of the Divine—it must be a team deal, and it's going to play itself out as a conscious experience.

Here's more specific instruction to help us from Haanel's writings:

> When you come into possession of a sense of poise and power you will be ready to receive the information or inspiration or wisdom necessary for the development of your purpose.

Hopefully you're in progress already in learning how to "come into possession of a sense of poise and power." The key words in this quote for us now relate to the three inputs that you can receive from the Divine: information, inspiration, and wisdom.

Those are what you want to bring back from your immersion in the presence of Universal Mind during your meditations. And you do bring them back with you. It's so important to begin to fully accept the fact that your inspired thoughts do come from this deeper source beyond your personal bubble of awareness.

Every thought is received by the brain, which is the organ of the conscious mind. Spirit is omnipresent, ever ready; all that is required is a willingness or desire to become the recipient of its beneficent effects.

So a primary desire within you must be this desire to receive wisdom, information, and inspiration into your brain as a conscious thought or vision or realization or whatever. Do you truly hunger for an inflow from the Universal Mind into your personal mind? And if you do, how can you optimize the communication from the Infinite to your conscious awareness?

Let's dig into this deeply, because once again we've hit a step in this manifestation process where so many people stumble and fall. And again, let's look to the master for insight into this question of how and where do we receive inputs from beyond:

> We are related to the world within by the subconscious mind. The solar plexus is the organ of this mind. It is through the subconscious that we are connected with the Universal Mind and brought into relation with the infinite constructive forces of the universe.

This statement is true as you open up to make contact. It's also equally true as you consciously open up to bring the Infinite into finite expression in your mind. You have spent time way out beyond your mortal limitations, using your unconscious presence as your link with the Universal Mind. Now you must actively bring the desired wisdom and information and inspiration into your body, literally, and thus to your brain and into conscious thought.

The trick isn't to fixate your attention on your brain. Haanel insists that you focus instead elsewhere in your body, a particular location that functions as the receiver for the incoming broadcast from Universal Mind. I quickly mentioned this step in the introduction. Let me show you a key quote again because it will make much more sense here than it did earlier in this book:

> The solar plexus is the point at which the part meets with the whole, where the Infinite becomes finite, Universal becomes individualized, Invisible becomes visible. It's the point at which life appears, and there is no limit to the amount of life you can generate from this solar center.

That's a rather strong statement. And you will find this statement to be one of the most important in this book, because most people are simply looking in the wrong place, in their desire to receive insight from God to help them in their lives. They look to their hearts usually, but that's not quite where the inflow happens.

So what is the big deal about the solar plexus? It's a key chakra location in ancient Hindu tradition, and it's the center of power in the body and in the subtle astral system according to Yoga masters. We noted earlier that what you need in order to manifest is power. And the solar plexus does seem to be the center of power in the body.

The solar plexus is also the epicenter of your breath reflex. The diaphragm muscle is right in the middle of the solar plexus, and, as you have seen, deep breath awareness is the key link that shifts you from mundane thought into the Silence, where you receive insight and empowerment.

Already, in practicing the breath-awareness meditation learned earlier in this book, you've been learning to focus your attention directly toward the solar plexus, so this isn't a new experience for you; it's just being used in a different step of the manifestation process.

Before you say the next Focus Phrase to yourself, the crucial act is always to first make sure you're still aware of your breathing experience. Otherwise, you're simply not going to be plugged in, and nothing's going to happen in terms of receiving manifestation power and vision.

I hope you are staying aware of your breathing while reading this book, page by page. You can of course do everything in your life while also staying aware of your ongoing breath experience, and you'll do what you're doing with more inspiration and power. For instance, right now I'm writing these words while staying aware of my breath experience. That's my constant discipline for writing anything, because it allows Spirit to be right here writing this with me.

You can have Spirit right here with you right now as you read these words, not as an idea, but as an actual presence, a presence found . . . where?

Right in the middle of your breath experience.

Right at the center of your solar plexus.

Right . . . now.

CREATIVE AND INSPIRED THOUGHT

Each time in this manifestation process when you say to yourself the fifth Focus Phrase, "I feel connected with creative power," you are plugging in to receive. And in order to receive, please note that you need to shift your attention directly to the region of your solar plexus, located deep within the center of your torso, just below your heart.

Your mind is quiet. You're focused on what you deeply desire. You've temporarily surrendered your personal ego thoughts and opened up to receive inspired thoughts. Now, all you do is breathe into whatever comes to you as you remain focused on your solar plexus and your breathing, which are one and the same. And in this state of expanded awareness, you let Spirit come flowing into you and also radiate out through you into the world.

Infinite Life flows through you; is you.

Its doorways are the faculties of your consciousness.

To keep open these doors is the secret of power.

With your doors open, right here in this process is the moment when, as you keep your everyday mind quiet, you begin to experience the infusion of new ideas rising up from your solar plexus, into your heart, then into your throat and tongue, and into your thinking mind. You might hear your inner voice of wisdom speaking to you. You might see a vision of what you want to accomplish. You might flash with a realization of your higher purpose. You might move into a flow of inspired thoughts that come to you and become yours.

What's important is keeping the mind quiet so that Spirit can speak. And please hold in mind that insights often don't come right away. Sometimes you'll finish a session and nothing at all seemed to come to you, but then, as you're driving to work, or as you take a shower, or go for a walk, or begin to slip into sleep, suddenly, pow! You receive the full complete vision.

I hope you can now see why doing this short manifestation process often, at least once a day, is crucial to fulfillment. You must lead your horse to water, even though you can't make him drink. You must regularly bring your mind into the presence of Creative Power, even though you can't make inspiration happen on demand. You must become temporarily passive, receptive, silent, humble, and open, and, with your focus on your solar plexus and your breathing, let Spirit do what it wants.

Your ego self is temporarily surrendering to your higher infinite self. There's going to be plenty of time when the thinking, conscious mind is going to take the lead, as we'll see in the next chapter. But the conscious mind first requires the inflow and cooperation of the unconscious mind and its infinite spiritual link in order to gain the creative power and vision to act.

FINALLY, TIME TO MANIFEST

What's so special about Charles Haanel, as we've just seen, is that before he sends you into action to manifest what you need to fulfill your life, he requires that you first stop and move through the deep inner process described thus far in this book, so that you're charged with the power you need to truly change your life. Like my grandfather used to say, "Don't go hunting without first loading your gun." Don't try to manipulate the world with your personal ego power. Instead, choose to participate in the world with the infinite guidance and empowerment of natural law and spiritual help.

So often, people chase from one thing to another, getting this, then getting that. With their focus on short-term goals, they fail to establish the long-term vision that will lead them to lasting satisfaction. Each day, I am encouraging you to look inward to reaffirm your true purpose, your spiritually imbued vision, which will lead you step by step through all the various manifestations that create the full life you desire.

But how do you know what to do, right now, each new moment? How do you go from the perfect vision to the details of advancing your life as you so desire?

At this point, we come full circle. I began this book by asking you to learn how to quiet your thinking mind so that you can enter into the Silence and receive a vision based on your heart's deeper passion. Now I'm saying it's time once more to fire up the brain and get your mind in gear again. Remember: It's always a coordinated action of conscious and unconscious, between mind and spirit, that generates significant change.

> If we find wisdom in the world within, we shall have the understanding to discern the marvelous possibilities that are latent in this world within, and we shall be given the power to make these possibilities manifest in the world without.

As you use this book's manifestation process to tap into the "wisdom in the world within" and are therein "given the power to make these possibilities manifest in the world without," you reach the point each day where you are ready to apply your personal will to express the Universal Will:

As we become conscious of the wisdom in the world within, we mentally take possession of this wisdom, and by taking mental possession we come into actual possession of the power and wisdom necessary to bring into manifestation the essentials necessary for our most complete and harmonious development.

The key action here is caught in the words "become conscious of the wisdom in the world within." That's the "aha!" moment in which you experience flashes of insight, which in turn stimulate your thinking mind to begin to make plans that will lead to changes in your life that you desire.

But remember that your thoughts need to remain impregnated with the passion that underlies your vision. If you lose touch with the passion, you'll lose your power to manifest in positive directions. That's why it's so important each day to move through the manifestation process and again say to yourself, "I know what I want," and experience the core yearning that is empowering your mind's planning and actions.

Every day, go into the Silence and ask your higher self what you need to focus on and manifest. Find out where your passion lies in the present moment, and bring this insight and power back in through your solar plexus and thus up into your thinking mind, where it will "take possession" of the inspired vision and transform it into action.

INSPIRED MIND

Your mind naturally becomes active when it's inspired by a great idea. That's what passion does: It powers the mind. And with a direct link being kept open between the subconscious and the Creative Source, the thinking mind will be inspired with ideas of what to do each new moment to evolve your deeper dream into reality.

Many people make the mistake of thinking that the ego mind can generate all the steps along the path to fulfillment. This does not seem to be the case. The conscious mind is limited to its sensory inputs, to past experience, and to future projections based on past experience. Its creativity is limited to its personal knowledge.

But an inspired mind draws from the Universal Mind's infinite knowledge of what's possible, and therefore it can guide an individual person in directions the ego mind would never venture toward. That's why trusting Spirit for guidance each new day leads to greater fulfillment than letting the ego mind direct the show.

Your finite mind cannot inform the Infinite. You are simply to say what you desire, not how you are to obtain it.

When you clarify that deep down what you desire is a brighter, more loving, happier inner feeling, then the Infinite will guide your thoughts step by step each day in directions that help you feel that heightened sense of positive life and love.

This is the giant difference between the ego mind trying to manipulate the world selfishly to satisfy its lower-level needs and passions, and the coordinated mind choosing to participate in God's creation so as to create a truly more harmonious and happy world. Once you see the difference, you'll regularly choose the latter, because the payoff is vastly greater for all.

So I challenge you, each new day, to tune deeply into the Source. Listen to your inner voice. Bring wisdom and vision into your mind through your solar plexus. And then enjoy the rush as your thoughts begin to play with the vision and to imagine new game plans for actively improving the world and your role in the world.

CREATIVE CONSCIOUS THOUGHT

Once your mind has generated a vision of your ultimate aim and purpose, be it for a large or small aspect of your life, it's time to apply your inspired vision to the outer world. And the first step in this outward movement of creation is to inform your unconscious mind of your vision, so that all aspects of your personal being are working together to create the world you desire.

You have brought your vision into your conscious mind through your solar plexus and subconscious awareness. You have taken the inspired vision and consciously created ideas and imaginations of your intended goal. You have a perfect vision of what you want to do, and now you must broadcast this vision out into the world, so that by the Law of Attraction you will bring to you everything you need to manifest your vision.

How do you clarify to your subconscious mind and to the world around you what your vision is? Again, Haanel surprises us out of our habitual assumptions by stating that the conscious mind must now broadcast its intent out to the world, through the solar plexus.

> The solar plexus is omnipotent because it is the point of contact with all life and all intelligence. It can therefore accomplish whatever it is directed to accomplish—and herein lies the power of the conscious mind; the subconscious can and will carry out such plans and ideas as may be suggested to it by the conscious mind.

Do you know that wonderful creative feeling when you're in the flow, when everything is going right in your life, when your whole being seems to be participating in perfect harmony with the outside world? That's the feeling that comes when your conscious mind successfully broadcasts to your unconscious mind and to the world outside how you want to work harmoniously in a win-win world to create a new vision that came to you from God.

That's the same feeling of passion that you tapped into when deep in communion with your Creator. Now your passion is manifesting in the world. And that's why it's vital to regularly pause and regain your oneness with your higher desire to manifest an inspired vision in the world.

Once your thinking mind becomes impregnated with spiritual power and vision, that same thinking mind that was once perhaps fixated on negative attitudes and disharmonious thoughts becomes transformed. In its limited, conditioned, fear-based state, the thinking mind can be highly destructive and a master of self-sabotage. But in its awakened state, your thinking mind becomes the champion leader of a new vision. People will follow this leader, come together to fulfill the dream, and create a sense of community that lets Spirit fill everyone's hearts.

That's a beautiful vision—and it's what most of us want to participate in. When more and more of us learn to manage our minds so that we regularly tap into spiritual insight and guidance, that's the kind of world we can have.

> Conscious thought, then, is master of the solar plexus, from which the life and energy of the entire body flows. The quality of the thought which we entertain determines the quality of the thought which we radiate, which consequently will determine the nature of the experience which will result.

Which is to say, let's manage our thoughts and infuse them with Spirit, so that the quality of our thoughts broadcasts a positive vision.

LET YOUR LIGHT SHINE

We'll speak more of this theme in later chapters. It's now time to end the chapter by sharing with you a Focus Phrase designed to bring your focus directly to the perfect vision that has come to you in your manifestation process. Haanel insists that rather than fixating overmuch on the details of your vision (which will emerge step by step as you go about your day), continue to hold in your mind your perfect vision. Imagine the completed dream, hold this perfect goal strongly and with passion in your heart, and broadcast this perfect vision (which is more a feeling than a concept) out into the world through your solar plexus.

Here's the Focus Phrase that stimulates this process:

"My vision is right now perfect and complete."

Hold this thought in your conscious mind, speak it and broadcast it, and your unconscious mind will believe it, take it in, and act on it.

And with every new breath, breathe your vision out into the world!

I love how Haanel says this:

It is evident, therefore, that all we have to do is to let our light shine; the more energy we can radiate, the more rapidly shall we be enabled to transmute undesirable conditions into sources of pleasure and profit.

I can guarantee you that if you regularly say this Focus Phrase to yourself, if you hold your perfect spiritually imbued vision in mind and let this passionate light shine in the world, you will effortlessly begin to manifest this inspired vision in the world.

Are you managing to read these pages while staying aware of your breathing at the same time?

Let's pause again so that you can tune fully into your breathing experience and move through the evolving manifestation process that you're learning by heart step by step:

1. *"I choose to focus enjoyably inward."*

2. *"My mind is quiet . . . I am now in the Silence."*

3. *"I am open to receive guidance from my Source."*

4. *"I know what I want."*

5. *"I feel connected with creative power."*

6. *"My vision is right now perfect and complete."*

PART THREE

ACHIEVE GENUINE
FULFILLMENT

❖ 13 ❖

Apply the Daily Attraction Process

~⚜~

L ong before you read this book and considered consciously applying a daily manifestation process to boost your sense of success and fulfillment, you were already manifesting the world you live in. When you were a baby and you felt hungry, your body responded with the cry reflex, which brought your mother or father or other caregiver to you to satisfy your need. The act of manifestation is the core process through which you have survived every day of your life.

Now, as an adult, it's important to acknowledge that you're already fairly good at manifesting what you need. One way or another, you get up and manifest the money you need to pay for food and housing and other things. You work to manifest and maintain loving relationships. Same with good health and all the rest. Everything you see around you is caught up in your own manifestation powers.

How does this work? It's really very simple. You feel a need within you. You visualize what you imagine you require in order to satisfy that need or desire. Then—and here's the key of this chapter—you focus your attention concertedly in the direction that you imagine will supply the fulfillment of your need . . . right?

If you seek abundance of whatever kind—material, emotional, spiritual—you move through the process of attracting to you whatever you want. Haanel says this succinctly:

Abundance will not come to you out of the sky; neither will it drop into your lap. But a conscious realization of the Law of Attraction, plus the intention to bring it into operation, plus the will to carry out this purpose, will bring about the materialization of your desire.

If you are out of work and need money, you will feel this need acutely at some point. This inner emotional pressure will stimulate ideas about how to make money, and then you will act on this idea by going out into the world to manifest what you need.

It's the same with relationships. If you're lonely and hungry for love, you'll experience an intense yearning, which will stimulate a vision of the ideal relationship you want, which in turn will generate pragmatic ideas of what you need to do. Then you'll act on those ideas and begin to attract to you the person you hunger for. I've written extensively about this particular application of the attraction meditation process in *Let Love Find You*, and the principle and the process are the same here.

What we're doing in this book is raising into clear pragmatic consciousness all of the steps needed to truly satisfy your desires. Perhaps your ego mind conjures up an ideal sexual mate and you find that ego ideal, but the relationship remains unfulfilling. In this manifestation process, you will know that there are deeper steps to be made if you're to manifest a lasting relationship that meets your core desires.

Haanel's approach to all this is fundamental because, as we've seen, he challenges you to tap deeper than your personal ego so that you are guided not just by your individual life experience and programming but by a universal perspective on your needs. I've walked you through this process of quieting your ego mind, looking inward to your Source, tapping insight and guidance from the Infinite Mind, and then bringing this insight and creative power back into your personal consciousness, where it will stimulate your imagination and thoughts.

That's the masterful approach to manifestation, and it leads us to a primary question: What is imagination, and how can you put your imagination to work in your conscious mind, so that you have a clear ideal vision of what you want to attract into your life?

TAPPING THE POWER OF IMAGINATION

We've seen that for high-level, long-term results, your personal imagination must be stimulated by your inner passion and inspired by the guidance and wisdom of Universal Mind if you're to generate an ideal vision that will propel your life forward to satisfy your desire. Imagination is that infinite meeting point between individual and Infinite. Ideas just pop into your head out of the blue—that's imagination. Here's what Haanel says:

> Imagination is the light by which we can penetrate new worlds of thought and experience. Imagination is a plastic power, molding the things of sense into new forms and ideals. Imagination is the constructive form of thought which must precede every constructive form of action.

Note that imagination is a "power" that takes your present reality and generates something new from your available resources at hand. This is creative power! In order to manifest something new, you must construct in your imagination the ideal image or thought and then proceed with constructive action.

Over and over, Haanel insists that you must focus your attention diligently not toward the details of your vision, but toward the ideal vision itself, the imagination in your mind's eye. And you are to focus in the present moment upon your vision as if it were already complete—that's so important!

> We are first to believe that our desire has already been fulfilled. Its accomplishment will then follow. This is a concise direction for

making use of the creative power of thought—by impressing on the universal subjective mind the particular thing which we desire as an already existing fact.

You must experience your imagined ideal vision as perfect in your own mind, and believe that it is in the process of manifesting in the outer world. Hold true to your dream, as they say.

If you desire to visualize and manifest a different environment, the process is to hold your ideal in mind until your vision has been made real. Give no thought to persons, places, or things; these have no place in the absolute. The environment you desire will contain everything necessary; the right persons and the right things will come at the right time and in the right place. Natural laws work in a perfectly natural and harmonious manner; everything seems to "just happen."

But to work within and activate these natural laws of attraction, you must discipline your mind to focus on your vision constantly for as long as it takes for the outer world to respond to your inner dream. This means that you must focus your mind's attention over time upon your ideal intent, until you attract to your life the material expression of what you are imagining.

In order to cultivate the imagination it must be exercised. Constructive imagination means mental labor, by some considered to be the hardest kind of labor, but it yields the greatest returns. All the great things in life have come to men and women who had the capacity to think, to imagine, and to make their dreams come true.

The practical reason that I keep insisting that you develop a daily or even hourly manifestation practice is because imagination "must be exercised." It takes concentration over time to make your dreams come true. But please don't think that I'm asking you to do something that is drudgery. Just the opposite: I'm asking you first to get in touch with your core driving desire, which you already at emotional levels strongly yearn to focus upon, then to use that passion to motivate and animate your "mental labor" so that labor is a pleasure.

Concentration is much misunderstood; there seems to be an idea of effort or activity associated with it, when just the contrary is necessary. In true concentration you should be so interested in your thought, so engrossed in your subject as to be conscious of nothing else. Such concentration leads to intuitive perception and immediate insight into the nature of the object concentrated upon.

If you spend most of your time worrying about what you don't have, if you let your attention drift all over the place rather than holding it where it will serve you best, if you let your thoughts fixate on negative attitudes and emotions, then chances are high that you will not succeed with your vision.

Your primary personal power, as mentioned before, is your power of attention. You get what you focus on. My hope is that this book and set of online support systems will help you to manage your power of attention more effectively, so that you focus more often on what you want and less often on what you don't have or don't want. And what positive incentive will we be using to spur this focused attention?

The incentive of attention is interest. The greater the interest, the greater the attention; the greater the attention, the greater the action. So begin by paying attention. Before long you will have aroused interest. This interest will attract more attention, and this attention will produce more interest, and so on. This practice will enable you to cultivate the power of attention.

THE ATTENTION MAGNET

Charles Haanel insists that everything you need is already present around you—you're simply not focused on it, and thus not attracting it (through your power of attention) to become part of your life. Hopefully this book and process will help you focus and thus attract what you hunger for. Haanel points out over and over that nine-tenths of the work in satisfying your needs is done in your own mind, not in the outside world.

And indeed this is true—once you get clear in your head what you truly need to be happy, these external environments tend to appear almost miraculously. But it's no miracle; you've simply applied a deeper logic to the manifestation process. Rather than our ego presence going out and trying to grab what you think you need, your higher presence attracts what you need to you.

Let's take a closer look at this whole notion of attraction. Haanel says this about the inner dynamic of the process:

> In manifestation, your predominant thought or mental attitude is the magnet. The Law of Attraction states that "like attracts like." Consequently your mental attitudes will invariably attract such conditions as correspond to their nature. If you wish a change in conditions, all that's necessary is changing your thought; this will in turn change your mental attitude, which will in turn change your personality, which will in turn change the persons, things, conditions, and experiences that you meet in life.

And so we return to the most resonant notion that Haanel brings to our discussion: If we focus our desired vision not on outer manifestations but on the manifestation of a more positive, brighter, and more loving inner world, then the outer world will naturally respond positively, because indeed like does attract like.

The Law of Attraction will certainly and unerringly bring to you the conditions, environment, and experiences in life corresponding with your habitual, characteristic, predominant mental attitude. It's not what you think once in a while but your predominant mental attitude that counts.

So what is your inner dream? If you hunger for a new person in your life, what is the inner change that you hope that person will bring to your heart's experience? Go into the Silence and let your higher wisdom answer that question for you, not as a philosophical ideal, but as a feeling ideal. How do you really want to feel inside your own skin? Tap into that core positive emotion as an ideal vision and focus on manifesting that feeling inside you. Then that feeling will attract like people and situations that will express and nurture that feeling.

> Create the mental image; make it clear, distinct, perfect; hold it firmly in your mind and heart. The ways and means will develop; supply will follow the demand; you will be led to do the right thing at the right time and in the right way.

By focusing on manifesting an inner emotional experience rather than an outer material environment that stimulates an inner experience, you're again cutting to the chase rather than getting lost in details. You're clarifying that you want most material things because of how they will make you feel. And you're choosing to focus on first manifesting the feeling inside your own being, and then letting the Law of Attraction naturally bring you the outer expression of your inner feeling.

LOVE IS STILL THE ANSWER

I mentioned in the beginning that Charles Haanel made a gigantic leap in his understanding of the power of attraction in the universe when he directly equated the Law of Attraction with the power of love:

The principle which gives thought the dynamic power to correlate with its object and therefore master every adverse human experience is the Law of Attraction, which is another name for love. There is no getting away from the Law of Love. It is the feeling that imparts vitality to thought. Feeling is desire, and desire is love. Thought impregnated with love becomes invincible. It is the combination of thoughts and love which forms the irresistible force called the Law of Attraction.

What a quote! Haanel has given us the master key to the manifestation of fulfillment in our lives. Science has been busy for the last hundred years since Einstein proving that the universe operates on basic laws of attraction that hold everything from subatomic particles to galaxies together. Haanel is simply applying the outer laws to our inner lives. Love is the power of attraction that brings us what we need to be whole.

Haanel often uses the words "resonance" or "harmony" in place of "love," but they're the same thing, and deep down we feel good when we resonate in harmony with our own selves and with others.

And what determines if we are harmonious and focused on positive loving feelings or disharmonious and caught up in judgmental, fearful, antagonistic, or other negative feelings?

The key is to be aware of and utilize the Law of Attraction every day and as often as possible. Your mental attitude is the most important factor for generating happiness and abundance.

As we saw earlier, we can spend years in therapy and never really change our attitudes, unless at some point we simply make the choice to stop focusing on negative thoughts and beliefs and attitudes and judgments, and choose instead to take charge of our own minds and focus our attention toward a loving vision of who we are.

We are what we focus on. We evolve in the direction that we focus our attention on. We have the power to shift our focus of attention at will. The choice is always before us. The challenge is to remember to make the shift away from fear-based thoughts and imaginings toward love-empowered thoughts and imaginings.

Let me review what we've already learned from Haanel concerning the process for creating more fulfilling and loving inner environments in our own minds and hearts—a process that is also the basis of effective cognitive therapy and successful meditation programs. He says it simply. If you want to change your inner life:

> . . . hold in mind the condition desired; affirm it as an already existing fact. This indicates the value of a powerful affirmation. By constant repetition it becomes a part of you. You are actually changing yourself; you are making yourself what you want to be.

Over the next few weeks, as you regularly enter into the Silence and open up to insights into the quality of inner feeling you desire deep down to be happy and fulfilled, you'll begin to generate a powerful ideal feeling imbued with the attracting power of love. You'll come to know with great gusto what you really want. You'll feel connected with your creative power to manifest this inner atmosphere and environment based on love rather than fear. Your inner vision of your ideal emotional condition will become perfect and complete.

And you will be ready for our final Focus Phrase, which will evolve your entire personality and inner sense of emotional well-being in the positive direction you are choosing and focusing on. Here's the seventh and final Focus Phrase of this manifestation process:

"Each new moment is manifesting my dream."

INTENT AS A PHYSICAL POWER

For thousands of years, human beings in all cultures around the world have developed religions in which human thought can directly impact the material world. The power of mind over matter became generally debunked as traditional Newtonian science gained influence over people's beliefs. But recently, more and more scientific studies have demonstrated that focused thought can indeed impact the outer material world. A hundred years ago Charles Haanel certainly believed this to be true and based his entire manifestation process on that belief: Thought has power to impact the material world.

The underlying principles of subatomic physics state very clearly that the entire universe is one great resonant entity in which each tiny energetic particle in the universe is connected and influenced by every other particle. Indeed each particle is constantly moving back and forth from form to energy and interacting with the summation of energy fields surrounding it. The whole universe seems to consist of energetic bundles and waves that cannot be defined except in resonant participation with all other energetic bundles.

But how do human thought, desire, intent, and focus fit into this new scientific understanding of life? Traditional Greek philosophy dictated that thought is not a material phenomenon at all, and that consciousness operates in a different dimension than do material things. However, new theories in physics now insist that for the universe to work, there are indeed more than three dimensions at play—at least seven at last count.

Consciousness does seem to function both within the space-time continuum and also in other dimensions, thus our ability to tap into the Source that, by definition, as the Creator of the universe, operates beyond its physical manifestation. And the Haanel vision makes perfect sense in this expanded sense of the interplay of the material world and the more subtle dimensions that must underlie three-dimensional functioning.

Perhaps the most important research that demonstrates how your inner thoughts have the power to affect the physical world around you is the Princeton Engineering Anomalies Research (PEAR) of the last thirty years, now completed but still just beginning to impress our minds with its discoveries. You can visit the official Princeton website at www.princeton.edu/~pear to read more deeply into this important set of studies conducted by the Princeton Engineering Department, but here's the gist of the research.

Many hundreds of subjects were asked to sit for half an hour and focus their power of intent directly at a random number generator to see if they could will the machine to generate more ones than zeros. The scientists doing the study wanted to prove Einstein wrong in his statement that "the intent of the experimenter influences the outcome of the experiment."

To make a fascinating long story very short, the statistical data showed that the random number generator did in fact skew its performance in the direction the subjects willed it to skew. After more than ten years of trying to refute the data, the scientists had to admit that indeed the human mind somehow can muster a force as yet unidentified and change the performance of a very physical and trustworthy machine beyond any chance effects.

This was a massive discovery. They then did studies that for the first time proved that ESP is scientifically valid. One human being can focus on a particular shape or number, aim this mental image toward another person in another room, and influence that person's choice of shapes or numbers. Again, the power of focused thought and intent was demonstrated to influence the outside world, in this case another person's mental activity.

The head of PEAR, a conservative aeronautical engineer whom I knew personally when I was at Princeton, then expanded his study with the random number generator to see what happened when more than one person participated in a test study. The results were jolting and proved Haanel's assertion that love is a physical force in the universe.

When two unrelated people focused their attention at the random number generator, the effect was doubled. But get this: When two people in a love relationship participated together, the effect was tripled. They had more power to influence the outside world than two people who were not emotionally related.

I relate these facts because with this and related research now formally completed in the scientific community, each of us must now realize that we are indeed impacting the world around us with our focused intentful thoughts. When we think negative thoughts about a person and aim these thoughts with passion at that person, we're actually assaulting that person physically. Thus the need for a new sense of responsibility for how we employ our thoughts.

Furthermore, from Haanel's perspective, when you generate an ideal image in your mind and concertedly broadcast that ideal mental image outward, you are indeed impacting the outer world with your focused intent, and the outer world will respond predictably. This is a clear, demonstrated scientific model for how the manifestation process actively brings you what you purposefully intend to receive.

> If you have been faithful to your ideal, you will hear the call when circumstances are ready to materialize your plans, and results will correspond in the exact ratio of your fidelity to your ideal. The ideal steadily held is what predetermines and attracts the necessary conditions for its fulfillment.

So each day, pause to generate and reinforce your ideal, and broadcast it outward. Nurture the inner feeling you desire, and the world around you will begin to respond, not just as a foggy fantasy of manifestation power, but as a scientifically proven process in which you attract to you what you truly desire.

Affirm Your Inner Need

Let's finish this chapter by returning to the core affirmation that Haanel taught, because it will help you to focus on the inner attitudes and conditions that will then empower the outer environment that nurtures your inner reality. Here is the quote you read before; now you will understand its power more fully:

> The affirmation "I am whole, perfect, strong, powerful, loving, harmonious and happy" will bring about harmonious conditions. The reason for this is because the affirmation is in strict accordance with the Truth, and when Truth appears every form of error or discord must necessarily disappear.

If you regularly hold that basic affirmation in your mind, with those seven inner qualities that together generate the core positive feeling we call happiness, then you will actively step by step shift your focus of attention away from the negative, fear-based thoughts that pull you down to the positive, inspired thoughts that will attract everything you need in the outside world to resonate with your new inner experience.

Finally, here's Haanel's formula in a nutshell:

> Earnest desire will bring about confident expectation, which in turn will be reinforced by firm demand. These three cannot fail to bring about attainment, because the earnest desire is the feeling, the confident expectation is the thought, and the firm demand is the will. Feeling gives vitality to thought and the will holds thought steadily until the law of Growth brings the vision into manifestation.

So be it.

Your Daily Manifestation Practice

Now that we've reached the end of the formal training part of this book, my challenge to you is that each new day, at least once, you spend three minutes or more doing the seven-step manifestation process that you've learned from this discussion.

I also encourage you to return to earlier chapters at some point and reread the explanation of each of the seven Focus Phrases, so that you begin to internalize the deeper aspects of each statement of intent. The Focus Phrases are portals that direct your attention toward vast realms of inner experience—and like I said before, each time you say one of them, you'll have a new experience.

If you have an amazing experience when saying a Focus Phrase, be sure *not* to try to repeat that experience the next time, because you never will. Time moves on, each moment is unique, and it's the newness of the experience that carries the insight and power and creativity you're seeking in this program.

Each day you will have particular needs and desires that are prominent in your mind. Most of these needs and desires will be of the temporary kind: financial, interpersonal, health-related, and so forth. It's fine to focus on temporary material or emotional needs and to use this manifestation process to move you in the direction of getting what you want. But hold in mind that temporary needs and hungers reflect a deeper yearning for a shift in the overall quality and focus of your life, so tap your deeper Source for insight, inspiration, and creative power.

Most people tend to focus on external things and situations they want to manifest in their lives. But as we've seen, it's the internal attitudes and feelings that really need attention and advancement. So when you do the daily manifestation practice, be sure to give time and attention to quieting negative thoughts and reactions, and to nurturing positive feelings and attitudes, because that's the change that transforms your life.

As a training adjunct that can make all the difference in truly succeeding with this program, we offer free online audio and video guidance through the manifestation process, so that you don't have to make overmuch effort to remember and move through the process. This multimedia support ensures that, wherever you are, you can pause and gain access to guidance and support, plus stay up to date on new developments in this program and the ever growing *Tapping the Source* community. Just pause and go online, any time of the day or night, to enjoy streaming audio and video guidance. You can also download the video files to your computer and put them into your mobile phone to play on the go while commuting or at work. You can also burn a DVD version of the guided manifestation videos to play on your home entertainment system.

We've made this free online support and reinforcement system as effortless as possible so that your focus can remain more on the new experiences that come to you each time you move through the process rather than on discipline and memorization issues.

And so, here's the core method. Be sure that you master and include the three-step breath-awareness process in item 2 so that throughout you remain aware of your breathing, which, as we've seen, is the "awareness medium" that guidance, insight, creativity, and manifestation function within:

1. *"I choose to focus enjoyably inward."*

2. *"My mind is quiet . . . I am now in the Silence."*

3. *"I am open to receive guidance from my Source."*

4. *"I know what I want."*

5. *"I feel connected with creative power."*

6. *"My vision is right now perfect and complete."*

7. *"Each new moment is manifesting my dream."*

❖ 14 ❖

Discover the Secret of Giving

∽❧∾

Experts in science, economics, and ethics all agree—no one operates as an isolated entity in this world. Regardless of our needs, we satisfy them as we interact with other people. And the spiritual adage of the ages remains as relevant now as it was in the past: In order to receive, we must also give.

Haanel was vehement about the inclusion of active and eager giving at the heart of the manifestation process. Here's how he states this:

> We make money by making friends, and we enlarge our circle of friends by making money for them, by helping them, by being of service to them. The first law of success is service.

Often in the pursuit of selfish acquisitions and triumphs, people lose touch with the underlying reality that in order to receive, we must serve. Every job on this planet is one of service, from the president, executive, and general on down to the ditch digger, dishwasher, and janitor. We all get up in the morning and do something that benefits other people and receive income or other things in exchange for our service.

Haanel points out in the above quote that friendship is the core positive ingredient in our financial endeavors. Superficially competition might seem to be the order of the day in business. But in reality, most of us spend most of our time at work engaged in cooperative relationships. We might compete with another company, but we cooperate inside our company for the common good and shared success. And ultimately our entire world economy is one large organism that survives and thrives through cooperation and friendship, not through negative attitudes and hostility.

Perhaps I can best summarize Haanel in this manner: harmony, friendship, love, and happiness are the key ingredients in anyone's success. We make money (or any other article of exchange) by helping our friends make money, by serving them.

You can make a money magnet of yourself, but to do so you must first consider how you can make money for other people. Your greatest success will come as you are enabled to assist others. What benefits one must benefit all.

What truly makes you feel good? Unless your heart is seriously contracted, you'll probably admit that you feel good in your heart when you're helping someone. Greedy grabbing from other people just doesn't feel as good as friendly giving, does it? Of course you need to receive. But if you consider the act of receiving, you'll realize that someone else is giving what you need to you—that's key!

And of course the logic under the surface observation of giving and receiving is that we're continually giving and continually receiving, but very often, if we don't give first, and give willingly and happily, the flow through which we receive gets stifled and cut off, and we experience shortage and failure.

A generous thought is filled with strength and vitality. A selfish thought contains the germs of dissolution; it will disintegrate and pass away. Our greatest success will come as we recognize that it is just as essential to give as to get.

With this quote we're again back to the notion that giving isn't just a physical outer act. Giving springs from generous thoughts, and generous thoughts, being imbued with love and harmony, give us strength and vitality. Thus if we focus on giving with a generous thought behind the act of giving, we create the positive inner attitude that is essential to manifesting what we ourselves want to receive.

So as you do your daily manifestation process, please include in your focus not just what you want to receive, but also what you have and want to give. If what you're truly seeking deep down is a brighter, happier feeling inside your own heart, hold in mind that your vision will need to include not just the things and experiences you want, but also what you are going to give in exchange for what you receive.

> You will get only what you will give; those who try to get without giving always find the Law of Compensation relentlessly bringing about an exact equilibrium.

Avoiding Extremes

I've noticed that all too often people swing from the extreme of grabbing all they can to trying to kill off their personal quest for what they need themselves and focusing entirely on trying to be giving. The truth is that there must be a harmonious balance between giving and receiving. They can't really be separated, or the vitality of human exchange is lost.

> Self-denial is not success. We cannot give unless we get; we cannot be helpful unless we are strong. If we wish to be of service to others we must have power—but to get it we must give it; we must be of service.

The basic laws of science clearly state that nothing is lost nor gained in the universe. Rather, there is a constant flow of particles and energy circulating, but not ultimately becoming less nor greater. For an economic system to work, money must flow through all hands. Money is powerful when in circulation, which means when it is being given and received over and over.

It's the same in a successful relationship. Both parties in the relationship must regularly give their love and attention, and both parties must be open to regularly receive. The vitality of relationship depends directly upon the flow happening between two people.

So observe carefully over the next weeks and months, when you pause to move through the manifestation process, whether you are generating visions and intent and imaginations that are purely selfish, or if you're building into your ideal vision the constant act of sharing, of helping and serving those around you. Take time to contemplate your current attitudes about giving and serving, and in the act of contemplation, while plugged into your higher self, you'll begin to wake up to your full potential for generosity.

Again, let's look at what Haanel says:

> A generous thought is filled with strength and vitality. A selfish thought contains the germs of dissolution; it will disintegrate and pass away.

Rather than fixating upon just yourself in your vision, begin to expand your vision to include other people. To succeed with your plans, include others. Your plan requires participation with other people to succeed. So consciously begin to expand your vision bubble to include what you are going to give to other people in exchange for what you're going to receive.

Generous thoughts can exist only in the mind of a person who feels that there is plenty for all. You must perceive yourself as someone who has enough so you can give some away—so that in the act of giving, you stimulate the inward flow of what you want.

At the heart of all this is the notion that the Law of Attraction functions within the higher power of love. When you are feeling selfish and greedy, there is no love in your heart at that moment. In this state of mind you are sabotaging your own success, because you will have no power to attract what you need. This might sound simplistic, but in reality it is a profound insight that Haanel is laying out for us to reflect and act upon.

We will get exactly what we give, but we shall have to give it first. It will then return to us manyfold.

Many times Haanel states that we must first give in order to receive. This is important. So many people plunge into doing a manifestation method fixated only on their need to get something. Their passion seems to focus only on the need to change their lives in directions they think will satisfy them. But they directly violate core principles of manifestation right at the start, and so fail in their efforts.

Often when people start to realize they must give in order to receive, they give without generosity or love, and of course they don't end up getting what they want. Furthermore, people tend to think that all they have to give are things, but the reality is that what they really have to give are positive, loving thoughts that in turn generate positive feelings in the other person.

There are a great many gifts we can give to other people, just by radiating our positive presence outward in their direction. As we saw in the last chapter, our thoughts do radiate outward and impact other people's inner lives, as well as the physical world.

With this scientific proof in mind regarding what you have to "give to the world," you can begin to circulate positive thoughts and feelings as a primary "thing you give" in exchange for what you receive. As usual, Haanel says it best:

Giving is a mental process, because thoughts are causes and conditions are effects. Therefore in giving thoughts of courage, inspiration, health, or help of any kind you are setting positive causes in motion which will in turn bring about their positive effect.

Each moment of your day, as thoughts run through your mind, you're impacting the world. If you want to manifest your vision, you must begin to be more aware of all those thoughts that you're broadcasting, otherwise you're directly thwarting your success.

Please take time over the next weeks to reflect upon this primal aspect of success in life. Every moment, as thoughts move through your mind, you are determining your fate. And you do have the power to quiet negative thoughts when you get caught up in them.

Remember earlier chapters in which we talked about quieting the mind. All you need to do when you're caught up in negative thoughts is to turn your attention to the air flowing in and out of your nose, and expand your awareness to include the movements in your chest and belly as you breathe, and all thoughts will temporarily stop.

Once you've quieted your thoughts, it's time to go ahead and tune into your inner voice, tap your higher passion and vision, and then bring that vision in through your solar plexus and up into your mind. Lo and behold, you'll find yourself with brighter thoughts springing to mind, thoughts that carry positive feelings and intent that will positively impact those around you.

The quality of the thought which you entertain determines the quality of the thought which you radiate, which consequently will determine the nature of the experience which will result.

It's not just the thought itself; it's the quality of that thought that matters. And by quality Haanel means the emotional charge accompanying the thought. Almost all thoughts pack an emotional charge, which stimulates glandular and muscular experiences throughout your body. And it's that whole-body charge that radiates out and impacts the world.

So giving implies monitoring the quality of your thoughts and taking responsibility for quieting negative, fear-based thoughts and nurturing positive, love-focused thoughts. Your ego can't force or manipulate the feeling of generosity into your thoughts. But if you regularly pause and tap into your Source, you access infinite loving intelligence and power. That's what this is all about: receiving love from God and giving it to the world.

❖ 15 ❖

ACHIEVE ENDURING ABUNDANCE

❖

The opposite of abundance is scarcity, which is a dreaded word that makes people feel immediately anxious and stressed. When there isn't enough to go around, naturally we panic. And, truth be told, most people seem to chase after abundance because deep down they're afraid of and running away from scarcity, because, when taken to the extreme, scarcity ends up in starvation and death—the ultimate fear.

When we let fear be what drives us, we tend to generate fairly miserable lives because, as we've seen in this book, we tend to manifest what we focus on. If we're focusing on worries and negative images of the future, we're going to create situations that reflect our negative focus.

So the first step toward creating enduring abundance in our lives is to consciously examine any existing fear-based attitudes and images that we might be holding chronically in our minds, and then go into action to shift our focus from fearful to hopeful images and actions.

Haanel had much to say about fear and how fearful thoughts and images erode our capacity to mobilize the powers of positive manifestation that lead to abundance. For instance, reflect a moment on this quote:

The one archenemy which must be absolutely destroyed is fear. Fear hides the sun and causes a perpetual gloom; it must be eliminated; it must be expelled. When fear is eliminated, your light will shine, the clouds will disperse, and you will have found the source of power, energy, and life.

Of course, fear is so dominant in most people's minds and lives that it seems like wishful thinking to talk about eliminating and expelling fear. How on earth could we achieve this massive psychological transformation? This question has been a primary quest in my own work as a psychologist, and I am pleased to say that within the worldview that Haanel offers, there is the power and guidance required to put aside fear-based thoughts in exchange for positive, hopeful thoughts.

The only solution to feeling chronically anxious, from both a spiritual and a cognitive therapy perspective, is to choose not to focus on images that generate the fear response. Instead, we do have the power to hold our focus on positive thoughts and images. This does not mean that we hide our heads in the sand and go into denial of the dangers life inevitably throws our way. It simply means that we focus on positive solutions to the danger rather than fixating on horrid worst-case scenarios. Haanel describes this cognitive-shifting dynamic in the following words:

> Physically, two things cannot exist in the same place at the same time. The same is true in the mental and emotional world. Therefore the remedy to feeling timid, vacillating, anxious, and harassed by negative thoughts is to substitute thoughts of courage, power, self-reliance, and confidence for those of fear, lack, and limitation.

This might sound simplistic, but Haanel's hundred-year-old logic is exactly the same logic that cognitive psychologists have recently developed and acted on. We do have the power to focus on what we want to in our own minds. If we learn to employ that power, we can put aside the negative thoughts and images that generate an emotional fear response. We can "substitute thoughts of courage, power, self-reliance, and confidence for those of fear, lack, and limitation."

When you realize that you are one with the Infinite Power, and that you can consciously overcome any adverse condition by the power of your thought, you will have nothing to fear; fear will be destroyed and you will come into possession of your birthright.

Again notice that realization is always key in Haanel's formula for improving your life. And this realization is not an intellectual process in his understanding—it's a deeper spiritual process that comes to you when you pause, quiet your mind, and enter into the Silence.

Haanel suggests developing particular affirmations, or Focus Phrases as we're calling them here, that will accurately point your mind's deeper attention toward a specific intent you want to activate, in this case the intent of shifting your attention away from tense, fear-based thoughts toward peaceful, harmonious, positive thoughts. In my therapy practice I often teach the following Focus Phrase for this situation:

"I put aside all my worried thoughts, and feel confident and peaceful."

As mentioned before, when you create Focus Phrases for a specific intent, make sure you put into words exactly the action you want to accomplish in your mind. This is what successful mind management is all about. Here's how Haanel talks about this process:

The way to fight darkness is with light; the way to fight cold is with heat; the way to overcome evil is with good. To achieve what you require, make use of the appropriate affirmation. Take it into the Silence with you, until it sinks into your subconscious.

If every time you think about abundance you feel anxiety about not having enough, then you'll want to seriously delve into the power of this specific application of the manifestation process I've been teaching you. Most people are chronically caught up in worried thoughts and fear-based images of the future—don't feel you're alone in this. Just choose right now to begin actively refocusing your attention away from anxious thoughts.

> If you wish to eliminate fear, concentrate on courage. If you wish to eliminate lack, concentrate on abundance. If you wish to eliminate disease, concentrate on health.

INNER AFFLUENCE

Notice what happens in your mind reflexively when you think about affluence and how your life would change if you became truly affluent, if you had more than enough to sustain long-term happiness and confidence. Does your mind immediately imagine a big house, plenty of money in the bank and stocks in your name, protection from any and all dangers that might threaten you physically, and so on and so forth?

I suspect you know by now that building up outer wealth is no guarantee of long-term affluence, because there are many variables in life beyond material goods that determine whether you're truly affluent. I don't mean to preach an obvious observation. But so often we tend to overlook the obvious in our pursuit of a better life.

Especially in America we have been sold on the false assumption that money can buy us pretty much everything we need. But of course it can't, so when you enter into your daily meditation to activate the Law of Attraction and bring to you want you need to he happy, it's wise to consciously hold in mind what you truly yearn for in life.

We've seen that our outer world tends to end up looking pretty much like our inner world, especially emotionally. If we're caught up in hostile, fearful, negative emotions day in and day out, we tend to attract those like emotions and breed more anxiety and disharmony. So perhaps the big change in our lives is not the usual material affluence, but something far more trustworthy and lasting: inner affluence.

Affluence within is found to be the secret of attraction for affluence without.

And what does "affluence within" really mean? It means holding thoughts and images and emotions and visions within our hearts and minds that plug us into the Infinite Fountain of affluence—that's where genuine well-being is found.

Our permanent well-being will be best conserved by a conscious cooperation with the continuous forward movement of the Great Whole.

I love Haanel's choice of words: "conscious cooperation with the continuous forward movement of the Great Whole." The whole world is unfolding according to a long-term natural plan.

The ancient Chinese called this the Tao, or the Way, or the Flow. By whatever name, there is a natural unfolding taking place in the world, and you are a participant in this natural unfolding. If you focus on "conscious cooperation" with the forward movement of the Great Whole, you predictably will attain and conserve a quality of permanent well-being in your life.

From my understanding, the only way to consciously cooperate with the Universal Mind's unfolding is to regularly pause and focus inward to tap guidance from the Creator. That's why the establishment of a daily practice, as we're exploring in this book, seems to be the only logical path to walk if you want to walk the path of abundance.

BECOMING GENUINELY WEALTHY

Affluence means wealth. It means having plenty, so that you are not wanting. It means being plugged into the flow of goods and resources so that you're regularly refreshing your abundance even as you use it up.

I know people living utterly simple material lives who seem radiant with well-being and happiness.

Material wealth should never be desired as an end, but simply as a means of accomplishing an end. Success is contingent upon a higher ideal than the mere accumulation of riches, and he who aspires to such success must formulate an ideal for which he is willing to strive.

Let's once again make a list of what most humans need in order to feel a sense of well-being in all aspects of their lives. Each time you pause and move into meditation on manifesting what you yearn for, make sure you're covering all these bases.

Material Abundance

Money is of no value except to bring about the conditions you desire. These conditions are necessarily harmonious.

It's no fun to run out of rent money or cash to go buy the groceries. Let's not fool ourselves; money counts! On the other hand, a lot of money brings a lot of responsibility; you must pay attention to your money or you lose it, and you can easily fall victim to worrying about your money rather than enjoying it. So keep this desire for cash and possessions in perspective with the other three equal needs.

Relationship Abundance

Whatever you desire for yourself, affirm it for others, and it will help you both. You reap what you sow. If you send out thoughts of love and health, they return to you like bread cast upon the waters.

People who are friends to others find that they indeed have friends. Radiate love and happiness to those you encounter, and this love and happiness will be radiated back to you. True relationship abundance is both deep and wide. Ideally you have a deep resonance with family, and you and your intimate partner have broad goodwill toward those with whom you work, play, and interact on a daily basis. The Beatles had it right: All you need is love, and truly the love you give will come back to you many times over.

Health Abundance

Every cell in your body is intelligent and will respond to your direction. The cells are all creators and will create the exact pattern which you give them. Therefore, when perfect images are placed before the subjective, the creative energies will build a perfect body.

Everybody knows that, except for medical interventions, money can't buy back your health, and a great deal of health depends on nonmaterial variables such as the amount of stress in your life, the impact of negative thoughts and emotions on your health, and the underlying spiritual soundness of your beliefs and aspirations. Using the manifestation process to generate health abundance can be a vital aspect of this program. We'll talk more about this in the next chapter.

Spiritual Abundance

If you see only the incomplete, the imperfect, the relative, the limited, these conditions will manifest in your life; but if you train your mind to see and realize the spiritual ego, the "I" which is forever perfect, complete, and harmonious, then wholesome and healthful conditions will be manifested.

One of my main reasons in deciding to write this book and highlight the teachings of Charles Haanel is that he brought such a remarkable spiritual depth to the whole notion of manifesting one's dreams in life.

Highest happiness is attained through your understanding of and conscious cooperation with natural laws.

Haanel brought God and nature, Spirit and science, together. For him there was no separation of our individual consciousness and Universal Mind. Whereas so many later writers fixated on Haanel's Law of Attraction and affirmation process as a get-rich-quick trick, Haanel continually returned in his writings to the essential requirement of first becoming attuned to God's will, and then manifesting a personal vision in harmony and resonance with God's will.

In this spirit, I strongly encourage you to approach your daily manifestation process as an opportunity to regularly look inward directly to your Source, so that you can fill your heart with spiritual inspiration and guidance as you go into action to fulfill your individual needs and desires.

CONTINUALLY IN RELATIONSHIP

As we've seen, wealth and well-being can't really be separated from your interaction and cooperation with other people. Wealth is a flow, not an accumulation. And as Haanel points out repeatedly, generosity is the truly satisfying path to affluence, not indulgence in selfish greed. Furthermore, love is the core passion that motivates the power of thought. As Haanel said:

It is love which imparts vitality to thought and thus enables thought to germinate. The Law of Attraction is the Law of Love; they are one and the same.

How do the Law of Attraction and the manifestation process operate in finding and sustaining a deep love relationship? In earlier books such as *Finding Each Other, Sex and Spirit,* and *Let Love Find You,* I've written extensively on the psychological dynamics of using the principles and practices outlined in this present book to attract a perfect sexual mate and long-term life partner. The same principles apply to attracting a new business partner or even tennis partner. First you must move through the process that brings you into deep contact with your yearning and desire. You must ask for guidance and help in manifesting a person who meets your need. And then daily you must return your focus to that desire and intent, and broadcast your intent outward.

As we saw in the PEAR studies, you have the mental power to contact and impact people around you with your thoughts and feelings. There are lots of people in the world who are also looking for someone like you, people you naturally will be in harmony with when you come together. In *Finding Each Other* and *Let Love Find You* I told my own story of discovering a meditation that very clearly brought my wife and I together twenty-five years ago. It was like a true miracle, and the basic process I'm teaching you in this book is the process that brought us together.

Life is without question greater than we can even imagine. What Haanel encourages us to do is to cooperate with the infinite mystery in which our lives unfold. Wealth and well-being, pleasure and fulfillment are our birthright. If we let the power of love guide us in our manifestations, there is without question plenty for all.

Let's let Haanel end this chapter with his predictably clear and potent words:

Thoughts of courage, power, confidence, and hope all produce a corresponding state. All we have to do is let our light shine; the more energy we can radiate, the more rapidly shall we be enabled to transmute undesirable conditions into sources of pleasure and profit.

✤ 16 ✤

HEAL YOURSELF AT CORE LEVELS

ealth and wellness are issues for most of us, and material abundance can mean absolutely nothing when we're seriously sick. Therefore focusing on and manifesting long-term health must be a vital aspect of this program. How can you maximize wellness each and every day, and also regain your health if you lose it? This chapter is dedicated to exploring the answer to this question by showing how to modify the daily manifestation session into a regular wellness-amplification process.

We'll talk about what to do when facing a current health problem, how to help others in this regard, and how to regularly act to maintain your optimum health. We're also going to take a clear Haanelian look at how to manifest and move through the last phase of one's mortal presence in optimum spirit and health, while also surrendering to the inevitable full cycle of life on earth.

It's now well proven that the thoughts you chronically hold in your mind generate parallel emotional and physiological conditions in your body that either support good health or undermine it. You've perhaps read or seen news reports on how stress, anxiety, depression, or anger, when continued over time, progressively reduce your immune system's ability to maintain optimum health.

Long before medical evidence was compiled regarding the influence of thoughts and emotions on physical health, Haanel identified the root cause of emotionally generated disease:

When one's thought has been filled with envy, hatred, jealousy, criticism, or any of the other thousand and one forms of discord, certain vibrations have been set in motion that, if kept up, result in discord, in harmony and disease.

There are of course genetic and environmental factors also involved in disease, but the psychosomatic dimension is the factor that you can act upon and have immediate power to alter. Haanel stated his core wellness procedure thus:

When your thought becomes uplifted, progressive, constructive, courageous, noble, kind, or in any other way desirable, you set in motion vibrations which bring about mental, moral, and physical health.

So again we see that positive mind management is the key to emotion management, which is the long-term key to good health. When you are caught up too long in anxious or hostile thoughts about the future or perhaps guilt and grief about the past, you have the power to immediately redirect your attention away from negative, stress-generating memories, fantasies, and images and refocus in more positive present-moment directions, as we've seen already.

When you pause to move through a daily manifestation session, you are actively making this shift into a better emotional state, plus you can identify your desire for optimum health and then tap health-related insight and guidance from your Source so that your conscious mind can begin to visualize your ideal health condition.

Remember, however, that Haanel advises you to keep your ideal visualization within the realm of realistic scientific possibility. Many people make the manifestation mistake of imagining their bodies transformed into an unrealistic health state that violates all natural law. Haanel insists that the ideal image and condition resonate in harmony with your natural potential—otherwise you're violating the very Intelligence of the universe that will empower your movement toward optimum physical health.

The only real power which you can have is the power to adjust yourself to divine and unchangeable principles. You cannot change the Infinite, but you can come into an understanding of natural laws and adjust your thought faculties with the Universal Thought. Your ability to cooperate with this Omnipotence will indicate the degree of success with which you meet.

If you are seeking success in recovering from a disease, Haanel insists that you must adjust yourself to the principles within which the universe operates, which include biological principles. Because biological principles include a remarkable capacity for healing the body, you do have the power to "adjust your thought faculties" and cooperate with your natural healing power.

Within the Haanel vision, you carry the ability to make remarkable recovery from illness. But you must tap your passion for recovery and draw on the Universal Mind's deeper healing power steadily over time if you're going to activate your recovery potential. And you must construct a mental image of the perfect health you seek to regain:

Construct mental images that are scientifically true. Subject every idea to analysis and accept nothing which is not scientifically valid. When you do this you will attempt nothing but what you know you can carry out, and success will crown your efforts.

CELLULAR INTELLIGENCE

As biochemistry affirms, right now there are billions of specialized cells in your body that have no great conscious overview of your body as a whole, yet they are functioning in perfect harmony and resonance and coordination with all the other cells in your body in order to keep you alive and healthy. This natural cellular intelligence and cooperation is one of the truly amazing phenomena of life in the universe.

> Every cell in your body is intelligent and will respond to your direction. The cells are all creators and will create the exact pattern which you give them. Therefore, when perfect images are placed before the subjective, the creative energies will build a perfect body.

We've been exploring in this book how you can create an ideal image of whatever you want. Broadcast this desired image from your conscious mind down through your solar plexus, and plug your driving intent into the infinite unconscious Spiritual Intelligence that includes each cell in our body. Hold the ideal in your mind with passion and hope and love, and the healing process is maintained in motion.

Let's listen to Haanel's discussion on cellular intelligence and metaphysical healing:

> All your cells are moving for a common purpose, and each one is not only a living organism but also has sufficient intelligence to enable it to perform its necessary duties. It is also endowed with sufficient intelligence to conserve energies and perpetuate its own life. This is the scientific explanation for metaphysical healing, and it will enable anyone to understand the principle upon which this remarkable phenomenon rests.

Again remember that Haanel does not expect you, nor advise you, to try to visualize the specific step-by-step healing process that your cells are going to move through to help you regain optimum health. Rather, he insists that you turn your focus with passion to the ideal image in your mind that you want to manifest as a physical reality in the outer material world.

Your expectation determines everything. If you expect nothing, you shall have nothing; if you demand much, you shall receive the greater portion. The world is harsh only as you fail to assert yourself.

And how do you assert yourself? Through pausing for just a few minutes, many times a day, to move through the manifestation process and reaffirm your intent and your specific ideal image as your dominant thought activity in your conscious mind.

You want to believe utterly in your perfect inner reality and broadcast this perfection out to your cellular presence, so that beyond your conscious awareness the infinite unconscious power of the universe can be working to heal you. And if you are currently healthy, regularly tap into your desire to stay healthy and broadcast this desire and inner faith and harmony to your cellular level of being:

Inner harmony is the foundation of health. The knowledge of your ability to consciously radiate health, strength, and harmony will bring you into a realization that there is nothing to fear, because you are in touch with Infinite Strength.

FEAR ITSELF

I've recently been working with hospices to bring the power of Focus Phrases to people in the last phase of life on this planet. From a therapist's perspective, the vast majority of our population is in serious denial about their own impending death. Rather than holding the full biological scope of birth, life, and death in mind as the complete progression of human experience, we tend to fight against rather than surrender to the natural path of life.

My professional observation is that trying to run away from one's own ultimate demise generates chronic anxiety. We know deep down that we're going to die, yet we try to fool ourselves into thinking we're going to live forever. In the process, we fail to develop a relationship with our own death and make death an enemy rather than our final friend who completes our human journey.

Hospice is a wonderful service because it offers people help in making peace with their own coming death, and helps to make the dying experience low on fear and high on acceptance and surrender. As long as a person is fighting death, this struggle keeps the soul in a very negative reactionary condition and the emotions thrashing around in the ultimate ego fear: that of the biologically grounded brain and personality ceasing to exist.

It is important for all of us, regardless of age or health, to learn to come to peace with the cycle of life and death. I hope you'll consider how the manifestation process can be used to help you come into touch with your infinite self through connecting with your Source regularly. This is of course what meditation is all about, and why meditation can ease fears of death so dramatically. When the ego regularly experiences communion with the Divine, it matures, lets go of its fantasy of eternality, and opens up to whatever comes beyond death.

The key is to be realistic in your intent. I don't mean to deny any religious belief about life after death, only to point out that we really don't know what's going to happen, so it's best to accept the biological truth that your body is going to cease to exist, whatever might happen at deeper spiritual levels. By preparing the ego (which is indeed a biochemical brain function of the body) for its ultimate demise, a great deal of core anxiety can be relieved, which in turn will improve your overall physical health dramatically.

You can begin to develop your ideal image of how you want to experience the last days of your life. You can manifest whatever kind of final-days experience you desire, as long as your desire and ideal image are in harmony with the laws of nature. Again, let's return to what Haanel says in this regard:

> Construct mental images that are scientifically true. Subject every idea to analysis and accept nothing which is not scientifically valid. When you do this you will attempt nothing but what you know you can carry out, and success will crown your efforts.

In sum, chronic fear-based thoughts and images erode your health. When analyzed carefully, it seems clear psychologically that the core fear that underlies all other fears is the fear of your own death, of your inevitable mortal demise. If you begin to nurture a realistic positive image of your own final days, you can defuse a great deal of your anxiety, which will directly boost your well-being. Please reflect upon this logic and use the manifestation process to regularly advance your positive relationship with your coming death. You can't avoid it, but you surely can make the process vastly more acceptable and spiritually valuable.

Helping Others Heal

A great many people, especially those who are parents, tend to worry chronically about the health and well-being of other people. What's really going on here? Does it help to worry about someone else, or does it actively push them in the direction of the worry? Furthermore, can positive focusing on another person help them heal?

We saw with the PEAR studies that our thoughts and projected intent, when aimed at another person, definitely impact that person at material and thought levels. (I encourage you again to visit the site that explains this research if it's new to you, because this will help you with the scientific analysis that Haanel was just talking about: You can indeed include thought power as part of your ideal image and intent.)

If you worry about someone's health and well-being, you're broadcasting that negative, fear-based image out at that person, and from my understanding, it will actually push that person in the feared direction. So there is even responsibility to consider here: You are impacting the world with your negative thoughts. Once you realize this, you'll have the desire to stop doing this.

Instead, you can tap your passion to help someone you love to attain better help by moving through the manifestation process to where you're holding an ideal image of this person's healthy body in your mind and projecting this out to the universe to respond to. One of my colleagues, Larry Dossey, MD, has written several books that offer a review of the scientific proof that prayer, when used in this basic formula, does provoke significant improvement in healing. But, curiously, it was found that the more specific your prayer, the less effective the prayer was. Just generally praying for a positive health condition was most effective, as Haanel would predict.

> If you desire to help someone, the correct method is not to think specifically of the person whom you wish to help; the intention to help them is entirely sufficient, as this puts you in mental touch with the person. Then drive out of your own mind any belief of lack, limitation, disease, danger, difficulty, or whatever the trouble might be. As soon as you have succeeded in doing this, the result will have been accomplished, and the person will be free.

What's essential in this process of helping someone heal is your preparation: pausing, quieting your mind, entering into the Silence, focusing on your passion to help the person heal, and then holding the ideal image of health for that person in your mind—regularly, over and over again.

In fact, as with other dimensions of manifestation, you will learn to take your ideal image and passion with you after the session, so that all day long your mind is holding the ideal image and broadcasting this ideal outward.

But hold in mind that this broadcast happens only when you maintain a core focus of attention down in your breathing, in your solar plexus. That's where your passion that will empower your visualization is found. Breath is the vehicle that moves your vision into manifestation. Then, with every new breath, you will be radiating health toward your sick friend.

> Every time you breathe, you breathe life, love, and spirit. This "breath of life" is the essence of the "I am." It is pure "Being" or Universal Substance. Your conscious unity with it enables you to localize it, and thus exercise the powers of this creative energy.

Wellness and Healing Focus Phrases

In addition to moving often through the manifestation process to aim healing power wherever needed, there are specific Focus Phrases that you can hold in mind all day to help you move in the direction of less fear of dying and more focus on wellness and healing.

For instance, if you find that you are indeed caught up in chronic worries or denial about your own coming demise, you can say to yourself often:

> *"I surrender to my own coming death."*

If you are currently sick and want to boost your healing potential, you can say to yourself:

> *"I am becoming more healthy with each new breath."*

If you know someone who needs to heal, you can say:

> *"I am sending healing energy to my friend."*

And if you want to communicate to your own cells your intent and desire to remain optimally healthy, say often to yourself:

"I am manifesting perfect health."

And once again, as a brief refresher, here's the full daily manifestation process that you're currently learning by heart. Be sure to also use the online guidance for mastering this process.

1. "I choose to focus enjoyably inward."

2. "My mind is quiet . . . I am now in the Silence."

3. "I am open to receive guidance from my Source."

4. "I know what I want."

5. "I feel connected with creative power."

6. "My vision is right now perfect and complete."

7. "Each new moment is manifesting my dream."

❖ 17 ❖

RADIATING SPIRITUAL INTENT

❧❧❧

We've seen that becoming engaged in the act of manifestation makes sense only when we currently possess an emotive charge, a yearning, or a need that's under pressure inside us and that we long to satisfy. Take away the need, the frustration with present circumstances, and the pressure for change, and human beings tend to ease up and do nothing at all. We shift from doing to being.

But, curiously, most of us seem to possess a lifelong longing to feel more connected with a higher spiritual presence, which we often call God. Haanel refined our deistic terminology in the following way:

> People have generally used the word "God" to indicate this universal, creative principle, but the word "God" does not convey quite the right meaning. Most people understand this word to mean something outside of themselves while exactly the contrary is the fact. God is our very life. The minute the Spirit leaves the body, we are as nothing. Therefore, Spirit is really all there is of us.

Haanel preferred to talk about Universal Mind, Infinite Creator, Creative Spirit, or the Divine, rather than using the traditional religious term "God." But by whatever name, as we've seen, the foundation of Haanel's entire manifestation process is based not only on the existence of an Infinite Creator who continues to actively permeate the universe, but also upon our communing directly with this Creator on a regular basis.

Writing a hundred years ago, Haanel was infected with the radical new writings and theories and worldviews of scientists such as Albert Einstein. He also seems to have been familiar with early English translations of ancient Eastern texts such as the *Tao Te Ching* and the *I Ching*. In later years he wrote in-depth books on yoga and Hindu meditation. So it was natural for him to use terms and philosophical concepts that reflected a break away from traditional Christian understandings and a tight integration of meditative and scientific notions of reality.

> The Universal Mind is the totality of all mind which is in existence. Spirit is Mind, because spirit is intelligent. The words are, therefore, synonymous.

Haanel placed individual consciousness on a par with Universal Mind. He experienced his own personal consciousness as a unified extension of the Creative Consciousness that manifested the universe itself, and therefore he saw human beings as tiny expressions of God, capable of actually demanding manifestation power from the Creator and receiving what they demanded. This reflects the Taoist and Hindu view of our relationship with the Creator quite closely.

> Mind is not individual. It is omnipresent. It exists everywhere. In other words, there is no place where it is not. It is, therefore, Universal.

What Haanel offers us is a pragmatic process for regularly accessing the Universal Mind and bringing its infinite creative power directly into our own minds, from where individual and universal operate in resonance to manifest the new.

We saw before that Haanel speaks often in words similar to those of Jesus when he gave the ultimately powerful challenge: "Be ye therefore perfect, even as your Father in Heaven is perfect." This perfect state of spiritual being is available to human beings upon request, and it's that perfect state that we are encouraged to focus on and envision in any part of our life that we want to improve.

> If you see only the incomplete, the imperfect, the relative, the limited, these conditions will manifest in your life; but if you train your mind to see and realize the spiritual ego, the "I" which is forever perfect, complete, and harmonious, then wholesome and healthful conditions will be manifested.

In my understanding of Haanel's teachings, you cannot tap into the manifestation powers that he's describing as your birthright unless and until you discipline your mind to temporarily stop focusing outward and focus inward toward the very center of your spiritual being. This is the meditative process through which you come into the presence of the Infinite Divine and through which your mind merges with the Universal Mind so that you are one and the same at that moment.

> The method for removing the cause of problems is to go into the Silence, and know the Truth. And because all mind is one mind, you can do this for yourself or anyone else. If you have learned to form mental images of the conditions desired, this will be the easiest and quickest way to secure results.

Again we have a parallel quote to one that Jesus is said to have spoken: "Know the Truth, and the Truth will set you free." The key term here is "know." As in Eastern traditions and science itself, just believing in something doesn't get the job done. What is required is actual experience, in which we move beyond believing to knowing that something is true.

That's what Haanel challenges you to do each time you pause and move through the manifestation process: to "go into the Silence, and know the Truth." And it is in this communion with the Universal Mind that you come to know if your passion or desire is truly what you need deep down:

> No matter what the difficulty is, no matter where it is, no matter who is affected, you have nothing to do but to convince yourself of the truth which you desire to see manifested.

I can't overemphasize the fact that the foundation of this manifestation program lies in regularly moving into the Silence and communing with Truth, with the wisdom of the Greater Intelligence. And again let me state clearly that you cannot enter into the Silence unless and until you practice sufficiently so you can quiet your usual mental chatter. This is accomplished through focusing on two or more breathing sensations at the same time.

COOPERATING WITH NATURAL LAWS

What happens when you quiet your mind, assume an inner meditative pose, and enter into the Silence? This is the most spiritual question one can ask, and of course words will not be able to grasp an experience that lies beyond words. But it is fair to say that when you quiet your individual mind and shift into receive mode, you will be able to directly experience insights that let you know the Truth. In the Silence, God can speak to you. You merge with the Godhead and thus know what God knows. This might sound like nonconformity from a theological perspective, but it's the mystic experience that lies as the foundation to all theology.

Haanel perceived the universe and its natural laws as the material expression of an infinite creation that we participate in when we merge our biological awareness with spiritual consciousness. Natural laws run the universe at both material and nonmaterial levels. And our lives must resonate in accordance with these natural laws if we're to express and also to advance God's creation through our personal lives.

Your highest happiness will be best attained through your understanding of and conscious cooperation with natural laws.

At the heart of Haanel's spiritual vision, there is both the core process of surrendering to God's natural laws and the process of coming into full conscious possession of your own vast powers.

As mentioned earlier, Haanel puts forth a fairly startling and from my experience entirely correct vision when he insists that the conscious individual mind is connected with the Universal Mind through our emotions and the unconscious dimensions of our personal consciousness.

It is through the subconscious that we are connected with the Universal Mind and brought into relation with the infinite constructive forces of the universe. It is the coordination of these two centers of our being which is the great secret of life. With this knowledge we can bring the objective and subjective minds into conscious cooperation and thus coordinate the finite and the infinite.

And once again, I quietly state the obvious: Only when you regularly move into the Silence do you gain the infinite spiritual perspective that enables you to successfully coordinate individual and universal in your own inner experience.

When you regularly turn inward and recharge your individual spiritual batteries by plugging into the Infinite Energy Supply, you not only empower and enlighten your own life, you also broadcast this spiritual radiance outward into the world around you, touching every heart.

Your Daily Practice

And so we come to the essential question of this book. I've shared with you a process through which you can manifest anything in your life that resonates with your deeper needs. You now know the basic theory as well as practice for this process. The book is coming to an end quite soon. When you close this book, are you going to discipline your mind's focus of attention to where you regularly take perhaps five or ten minutes a day to activate your higher creative potential and incorporate a daily manifestation program in your routine?

I am giving you cognitive tools that you can use to improve your life. Watch yourself the next few weeks, and be conscious of what you do or do not do. From that self-observation will come all you need to choose your course of action or inaction.

The manifestation process can be moved through in just a few minutes. You can do a short version of the process several times a day, which is highly recommended. You can also devote perhaps fifteen to twenty minutes or more once a day to move through a more in-depth manifestation meditation. This in-depth meditation can become your core spiritual practice if you find that you are longing for this depth of communion with the Divine.

REINFORCEMENT AND SUPPORT

This book comes with its own support website (www.tappingdaily.com), where you can receive free audio and video guidance through the core daily manifestation process. Letting me guide you through the process via media inputs is not cheating in terms of discipline; it's a valuable extension of this written guidance you have in hand, in a format that has been found ideal for training a new cognitive process. By not only reading but hearing the guidance, you can let go of self-discipline and shift into total experiential mode. This has proven of great value.

You will reach a point after a few weeks of working with this book and the online training programs where suddenly you realize you've internalized the seven-step manifestation process. That's what we're aiming for in the training.

Because each moment is new by definition, you'll always have a new experience each time you go through the process. The process is a portal leading you into infinite experience. Move through the portal into ever-expanding experience.

1. *"I choose to focus enjoyably inward."*

2. *"My mind is quiet . . . I am now in the Silence."*

3. *"I am open to receive guidance from my Source."*

4. *"I know what I want."*

5. *"I feel connected with creative power."*

6. *"My vision is right now perfect and complete."*

7. *"Each new moment is manifesting my dream."*

✩ PART FOUR ✩

PRACTICE
MAKES PERFECT

❖ 18 ❖

FINAL WORDS FROM CHARLES HAANEL

❧❧❧

We never reach a point in our lives where we don't need to continue manifesting the world we need in each new moment. It's an ongoing daily process. Even if you reach the point spiritually where you have few material desires or emotional yearnings and feel satisfied deep down, you'll still want to return to the Silence for insight and wisdom, as well as the power to broadcast positive healing vibes out into the world as your ongoing gift and contribution. So, one more time: Be sure to make the process of tapping into your manifestation Source a new essential habit in your daily routine.

I've now come to the end of what I want to say in this book, and I feel the desire to end this discussion by offering you a final immersion in pure Haanel wisdom. I might mention that I have taken the editorial liberty throughout this book of slightly modifying Haanel's quotes so that they read smoothly, are in the same tense as the manuscript, and communicate just one thought per paragraph. I initially went through the entire document and selected what seemed to be the best 20 percent of his writings for this book. Then I did minimal line editing so that the quotes read easily without any outdated terminology. In this way, I translated his hundred-year-old quotes into our current wording and punctuation.

And now, in the same spirit that I've been offering psychological and spiritual commentary upon Haanel's seminal paragraphs throughout this book, it's now your turn to read what we consider some core direct quotes from Haanel and experience your own insights and reflections. Some of the following quotes are ones you've already read that beg further reflection; others will be new to you.

First, be sure to take a minute or so to pause and enter into the Silence. Then, as you stay tuned into your breath experience (which connects you with deeper insight), read a quote and be open to whatever inner flashes of realization emerge effortlessly from your Source after reading that quote. Listen to your own inner voice, and enjoy!

❖

If you wish to express abundance in your life, you can afford to think abundance only, and as words are thoughts taking form, you must be especially careful to use nothing but constructive and harmonious language, which, when finally crystallized into objective forms, will prove to your advantage.

❖

Whatever you desire for yourself, affirm it for others, and it will help you both. You reap what you sow. If you send out thoughts of love and health, they return to you like bread cast upon the waters.

❖

Always concentrate on the ideal as an already existing fact; this is the germ cell, the life principle which goes forth and sets in motion those causes which guide, direct, and bring about the necessary relation, which eventually manifest in form.

❖

Thought constantly, eternally is taking form, is forever seeking expression. If your thought is weak, critical, destructive, and negative generally, it will manifest in your body as fear, worry, and nervousness; in your finances as lack and limitation; and in discordant conditions in your environment. If your thought is powerful, constructive, and positive, this will be plainly evident in the state of your health, your business, and your environment.

❖

Concentrate only upon the things you desire. Thought is creative. When you meet with success, gain, or any other desirable condition, you will naturally concentrate upon the effects of these things and thereby create more, which leads to even more.

❖

Abundance will not come to you out of the sky; neither will it drop into your lap. You must focus on the Law of Attraction and the intention to bring this law into operation.

❖

The affirmation "I am whole, perfect, strong, powerful, loving, harmonious, and happy" will bring about harmonious conditions. The reason for this is because the affirmation is in strict accordance with the Truth, and when Truth appears every form of error or discord must necessarily disappear.

❖

Successful people hold in their minds the ideal of the condition they wish to realize. They constantly bring to mind the next step necessary to manifest their ideal. Thoughts are the materials with which they build, and the imagination is their mental workshop.

❖

Imagination is the matrix in which all great things are fashioned. An ideal steadily held is what predetermines and attracts the necessary conditions for its fulfillment. Mind is the ever-moving force with which you secure the persons and circumstance necessary to build your success structure.

❖

Through a powerful statement of intent, hold in mind the condition desired; affirm it as an already existing fact. This indicates the value of a powerful affirmation. By constant repetition it becomes a part of you. You are actually changing yourself; you are making yourself what you want to be.

Make a mental image of physical perfection; hold it in the mind until it is absorbed by your consciousness. If the desire is one which requires determination, ability, talent, courage, power, or any other spiritual power, these are necessary essentials for your picture. Build them in. They are the vital part of the picture; they are the feeling which combines with thought and creates the irresistible magnetic power which draws the things you require to you.

❖

When the conscious mind is certain that a thought is true, that thought is sent to the subjective mind to be made into flesh, to be brought forth into the world as reality. Impress on the universal subjective mind the particular thing which you desire as an already existing fact. Believe that your desire has already been fulfilled; its accomplishment will then follow.

❖

If you wish harmonious conditions in your life, you must develop a harmonious mental attitude. And in order to possess vitality your inner thought must be impregnated with love. Love is a product of the emotions; therefore, let your emotions be controlled and guided by intellect and reason.

❖

The first form which thought will find is language, or words. This determines the importance of words; they are the first manifestation of thought. Thought may lead to action of any kind, but whatever the action, it is simply the thought attempting to express itself in visible form.

❖

Insight enables you to plan properly and to turn your thought and attention in the right direction, instead of into channels which will yield no possible return.

❖

The most commonly accepted definition of wealth is that it consists of all useful and agreeable things which possess exchange value. It is this exchange value which is the predominant characteristic of wealth.

❖

The power to create depends entirely upon spiritual power. Therefore the successful businessperson is more often than not an idealist ever-striving for higher and higher standards.

❖

You have the power to form your own mental images, regardless of the thoughts of others, regardless of exterior conditions and environments. By exercising this mental power and freedom you can control your own destiny, body, mind, and soul.

❖

In the last analysis, thinking is the one great cause in life. To control thought is to control circumstances, conditions, environment, and destiny.

❖

If you desire to visualize and manifest a different environment, the process is to hold your ideal in mind until your vision has been made real. Give no thought to persons, places, or things; these have no place in the absolute. The environment you desire will contain everything necessary; the right persons and the right things will come at the right time and in the right place.

❖

What you visualize already exists in the spiritual world; this visualization is a substantial token of what will one day appear in the objective world, if you remain actively faithful to your ideal.

❖

Imaginative visualization forms impressions on the mind, and these impressions in turn form concepts and ideals. They in turn are the plans from which your vision turns into material form.

❖

There is but one sense, the sense of feeling. All other senses are modifications of this one sense. Feeling is the fountainhead of power. This is why you must put feeling into your thought if you wish results. Thought and feeling are the irresistible combination.

❖

Construct mental images that are scientifically true. Subject every idea to analysis and accept nothing which is not scientifically valid. When you do this you will attempt nothing but what you know you can carry out, and success will crown your efforts.

❖

If you desire material possessions of any kind, your chief concern should be to acquire the mental attitude which will lead to the result desired. This mental attitude is generated by a realization of your spiritual nature, and your unity with the Universal Mind which is the substance of all things.

❖

Become so interested in thinking about what you desire, so engrossed in your subject that you are conscious of nothing else. Such concentration leads to intuitive perception and immediate insight into the nature of the object concentrated upon.

❖

Concentration does not mean mere thinking of thoughts, but the transmutation of these thoughts into practical values. Fundamentally the subconscious is omnipotent; there is no limit to the things that can be done when it is given the power to act.

❖

Your degree of success is determined by the nature of your desire. If the nature of your desire is in harmony with natural law or the Universal Mind, it will gradually emancipate the mind and give you invincible courage.

❖

You will get only what you give; those who try to get without giving always find the Law of Compensation relentlessly bringing about an exact equilibrium.

❖

Cultures are continually making progress in the methods which they use to come into communication with the Universal Mind and its infinite possibilities.

❖

Begin by paying attention. Before long you will have aroused interest. This interest will attract more attention, and this attention will produce more interest, and so on. This practice will enable you to cultivate the power of attention.

❖

You must "be" before you can "do," and you can "do" only to the extent to which you "are," and so what you do will necessarily coincide with what you "are"—and what you are depends upon what you "think."

❖

Large ideas have a tendency to eliminate all smaller ideas so that it is well to hold ideas large enough to counteract and destroy all small or undesirable tendencies. This is one of the secrets of success: Think big thoughts. The creative energies of mind find no more difficulty in handling large situations than small ones.

❖

If you wish a change in conditions, all that's necessary is changing your thought; this will in turn change your mental attitude, which will in turn change your personality, which will in turn change the persons, things, conditions, and experiences that you meet in life.

❖

And once again, here are your Focus Phrases:

1. *"I choose to focus enjoyably inward."*

2. *"My mind is quiet . . . I am now in the Silence."*

3. *"I am open to receive guidance from my Source."*

4. *"I know what I want."*

5. *"I feel connected with creative power."*

6. *"My vision is right now perfect and complete."*

7. *"Each new moment is manifesting my dream."*

AFTERWORD

So here you are. You've come to the end of this amazing book. I consider this an amazing book because it is so simple and yet so profound. True happiness is about so much more than material abundance. In working with and speaking to hundreds of thousands of people throughout my life, I know that what has given me most joy is not the acclaim and material comforts I have generated for myself and my family, but the inspiration and sense of hope and purpose that I have given to others. It has been a true blessing to be able to help lift others up, and I feel honored to have been asked to write the afterword for *Tapping the Source*, for it too is a work that is dedicated to helping others and sharing the practical secrets of how to make this a better world.

Many books contain uplifting stories and good practical advice. What is so special about *Tapping the Source* is that you now have an easy-to-follow series of Focus Phrases that you can use five to ten minutes a day for the rest of your life. Think of it as stretches you would do before doing physical activity to be sure that your body is ready for action. These are mental stretches, if you will, that will ensure that you stay focused on what matters and not allow the distractions of the outer world to bruise or injure your mental and emotional body. Haanel was one of the first great Western thinkers to clearly see that your emotional and mental body was as important as your physical body. *Tapping the Source* has taken this wisdom to the next level. Use this book daily. Share it with friends.

Two of my favorite quotes from Charles Haanel's *Master Key System* are "Concentrate only upon the things you desire" and "You reap what you sow. Send out thoughts of love." The focus phrases in *Tapping the Source* will allow you to increase your ability to concentrate upon the things you desire and send out thoughts of love. I guarantee you that you will start to see a difference in your life just from doing these simple mental stretches five minutes a day. And when you do, you will be amazed by what you create for yourself and those you love.

With my fondest wishes for your success and happiness,

Jack Canfield

ACKNOWLEDGMENTS

John Selby would like to acknowledge his wife and film partner, Birgitta Steiner, for her spiritual inspiration, creative insight, and ongoing support while writing this book and producing the related Manifesting Your Core Desires video training programs.

William Gladstone and Richard Greninger would like to acknowledge their families, including Gayle Newhouse and Carol Ryckoff, who have supported them throughout the writing of this book. Thanks also to Sterling editor Kate Zimmermann and editorial director Michael Fragnito, as well as Marcus Leaver, president of Sterling Publishing.

In addition the authors would like to acknowledge personal communications from the following authors, friends, and associates, all of whose communications have enhanced both the book and the accompanying feature film *Tapping the Source*:

Patricia Aburdene, Marc Allen, Dennis Andres, Aunty Angeline, José Argüelles, Bani Ashtiani, Janet Attwood, Collette Baron-Reid, Marty Birrittella, Rinaldo Brutoco, Connie Buffalo, Jack Canfield, Sam and Kate Cawthorn, Deepak Chopra, Richard Cohen, Michelle Cohen, DC Cordova, Barbara De Angelis, Chip Duncan, Hale Dwoskin, Crystal Dwyer, Jesse Dylan, Ehekateotl, Kamran Elahian, Arielle Ford, Linda Francis, Michael Gosney, Martin Gray, Jean Houston, Alexis Kaplan, Constance Kellough, Linda Kennedy, Harrison Klein, Sharmen Lane, Loral Langemeier, Ervin Laszlo, Barbara Marx Hubbard, Fred Matser, Sarah McLean, Drunvalo Melchizedek, Andrea Metcalf, Kristen Moeller, Sue Morter , Peggy O'Neill, Grandma Aggie Pilgrim, Debra Poneman, Sri Sri Ravi Shankar, Greg Reid, Gary Renard, Sonia Ricotti, Lucinda Ruh, Masami Saionji, Gerard Senehi, Marci Shimoff, Mark Sisson, Marilyn Tam, Eckhart Tolle, Alexis Traynor-Kaplan, Mark Victor Hansen, Victor Villasenor, Neale Donald Walsch, Marcia Wieder, John Woods, Gary Zukav

Additional Resources and Online Programs

Online Training, Inspiration, and Reinforcement

Most people tend to finish a book . . . and then forget to do the exercises even if they value them. For enjoyable effortless help in developing a long-term manifestation practice, please go to our TappingDaily.com website regularly. Enjoy our ever-expanding audio and video guidance and inspiration, plus chat rooms and forums where you can share with each other your experience with this program, while also accessing new short videos and written insights by the authors. From daily Haanel quotes to online seminars and special Source events, this TappingDaily.com site is your home for mastering the Daily Manifestation Process and participating in our *Tapping the Source* community. We will also be posting information about events on www. tappingthesourcebook.com, so visit both sites.

Advanced Coaching and DVD Programs

Also at TappingDaily.com you can learn about one-on-one coaching to help you manifest your specific dreams, as well as additional inspirational and training video programs available as DVDs, cell phone reminders, and computer downloads.

Live Seminars and Conferences

The authors offer special regional *Tapping the Source* seminars and conferences, which will be posted and described on www.TappingDaily.com. Tune in regularly to find out when there's a *Tapping the Source* event near you!

www.TappingDaily.com

and

www.tappingthesourcebook.com

READING GROUP QUESTIONS

This book is ideal for small groups to read and discuss in depth. The final pages of this book include a helpful guide for stimulating group exploration of this book's themes and manifestation methods. Here are twenty-four focus questions to reflect upon after reading this book:

1. A basic premise of the book is that there exists a Creator of the universe who permeates everyday consciousness and whose power and guidance can be "tapped into" at will by any of us. Do you agree with this?

2. The book's manifestation technique is based on the merger of psychological and spiritual understandings of human consciousness, where our personal bubble of awareness is able to connect with Universal Mind through entering the Silence and receiving insight and empowerment via the unconscious mind. How do you feel about this possibility?

3. Charles Haanel prefers not to talk about God, but rather to use other terms such as "Universal Mind," "the Divine," "Creative Source," and so forth. Do you agree with the spiritual premises of this book, or do they violate some of your religious beliefs?

4. The book mentions the PEAR studies, which seem to prove that the human brain does have the power to broadcast its intent and impact on the actual physical world. Did you examine the online evidence of this research? How do you feel about the implications of this study?

5. John Selby claims to have integrated cognitive science with spiritual meditative practice in developing the manifestation process taught in this book. Do you feel he succeeded in this merger of science and spirit? Or are the two so different that they cannot be integrated?

6. This book leans in the direction of deeper spiritual

dimensions of manifestation and human happiness, rather
than focusing primarily on the attainment of material wealth.
Are you comfortable with this focus on spiritual dimensions
of manifestation as being compatible with the practical
attainment of material desires? Why or why not?

7. Much of the book focuses on teaching a daily meditation
practice that touches the depths of both material and spiritual
needs and desires. Did you feel the book adequately taught
you the manifestation process? Have you been practicing this
method daily? What have been your experiences with this
process?

8. The first part of the process is supposed to help you quiet all
the thoughts running through your mind so that you can
enter into the Silence. When you focus on your breathing and
present-moment experience by using the Focus Phrases, do your
thoughts become quiet? What do you think of the whole notion
of quieting your mind so that you can listen to your inner voice
of wisdom and guidance?

9. Charles Haanel insists that your success in manifesting your
dreams must be driven not just by thoughts of what you want,
but also by your deeper passions and yearnings, by your positive
emotions. Do you agree with this? How well have you been able
to identify what your core passions and yearnings are?

10. The author talks about "shifting into receive mode" during a
manifestation session so that you can receive insight, guidance,
wisdom, and power to help you manifest your dreams. What do
you think of this process? Can you do it yet?

11. Charles Haanel says, "What you and I desire, what everyone
is seeking, is happiness and harmony." He urges you to aim
toward manifesting these two qualities of consciousness in your
life, rather than focusing on material things that you desire. Do
you agree with this, or is he being too simplistic?

12. In general, were you satisfied with the book's focus on deeper

spiritual aspects of fulfillment in life? After reading the book, are you clear about what you personally need to make you happy? Is happiness really what you want, or are you focused on something else?

13. This book insists that you must pay attention to your thoughts at all times and take responsibility for focusing your thoughts in positive directions if you want to manifest a satisfying life situation. Is it true in your experience that your thoughts always precede your actions? Do you feel you can take charge of your thoughts, rather than letting them run wild?

14. The Law of Attraction plays an important role in this book's manifestation process. Science has proven the physical Law of Attraction in atoms and so forth, but do you believe there is a mental and spiritual Law of Attraction as well? If so, do you feel you understand how to work with this Law of Attraction in your own life?

15. Another premise of this book is that there is "enough for all" and that abundance is something everyone in the world can experience. Is this just wishful thinking? If everyone in the world practiced this book's manifestation process regularly, would everyone be able to get what they truly need to be happy in life?

16. Charles Haanel and the authors of *Tapping the Source* have been called heretical because they see human beings as expressions of the Universal Mind, which means they're putting humans and God on an equal footing, with humans as material manifestations of the Infinite Creator. Do you agree with the authors? Are you actually able to tap into and channel God's power and wisdom into your personal mind?

17. Charles Haanel often stated that he was averse to all religion, and that his manifestation methods were based on science and spiritual insight, not traditional religious beliefs. But much of what he taught—for instance, focusing on giving rather than

receiving, and making love the ultimate true power—sounds like the teachings of Jesus. Was he just using new words to express traditional beliefs, or did he bring a genuinely new vision of spiritual life into being?

18. The use of Focus Phrases seems to be the driving force of this manifestation process. Did the book adequately teach you what Focus Phrases are and how to use them? Do you find them powerful and effective? Is it true that just by thinking a statement of intent to yourself you can generate movement toward what you want to manifest? Have you yet memorized the seven Focus Phrases that make up this book's method? What do you think of holding these Focus Phrases in your mind throughout the day?

19. Charles Haanel goes against the usual meditation grain when he insists that the solar plexus is the center of the human body and the point where Spirit flows in. Usually we think it's the heart or the mind, not the solar plexus. The book teaches that breathing is the core factor in awareness and manifestation, and that the solar plexus, which drives our breathing, must therefore be the key to manifestation. Do you agree with this? When you practice the manifestation process, can you focus down to your solar plexus? What do you experience?

20. The book talks about the necessity of changing your mental attitudes if you are to change your life for the better. Do you agree with this? Do you feel you can use the methods in this book to change your mental attitudes?

21. Power is also talked about, but with a particular Haanel twist that is different from the way most self-help and spiritual books treat it. Charles Haanel teaches that you must first go into the Silence and bring your personal intent into resonance and harmony with the laws of nature and Universal Mind's wisdom if you are to receive higher power beyond your ego's manipulations. Does this make sense to you? Do you want to do this in your life?

22. The book says that if you stay in conscious contact with your higher primary yearnings, each moment will manifest what you need in order to advance step by step toward your higher goal. Do you like this "higher vision" focus? Is it effective for you in also manifesting practical material abundance as well?

23. The book challenges you to use the free online training programs daily and to develop a strong daily habit of pausing to go into the Silence and tap your higher manifestation powers. Do you think you will discipline yourself enough to make this manifestation process a lifelong daily habit?

24. You can have the identity of a seeker and move on now to find more books that might hold the answers you're looking for, or you can see yourself as a tracker, and settle in with this manifestation method as your fulfilling process. Which do you think you will choose?

For further exploration of the questions, themes, and programs in this book, please visit www.TappingDaily.com.